Just Live It

Mary Barrett

iUniverse, Inc.
Bloomington

iUniverse books may be ordered through booksellers or by contacting:

iUniverse
1663 Liberty Drive
Bloomington, IN 47403
www.iuniverse.com
1-800-Authors (1-800-288-4677)

ISBN: 978-1-4502-9489-8 (sc)
ISBN: 978-1-4502-9490-4 (ebook)

Printed in the United States of America

iUniverse rev. date: 01/28/2011

Dedication

To my mother-in-law Betty Barrett, who celebrated each day the Lord gave her and showed me how to love Jesus, my husband, my children, and my home. You will forever be my Mother in Love that these books are named after. Your legacy of love for your family and your example of a Christ-centered life will be remembered through the generations of your children and grandchildren.

To my wonderful husband who has been my encourager and faithful partner. God has blessed me richly by the sharing of love I have with you.

To my sisters-in-law, who have worked so hard and also continue in faith to be a huge part of this journey. Thank you for being steadfast and believing in the mission and call of God in your lives.

May all glory and honor go to our Lord and Savior, who kept our feet on a clear path by His grace!

Contents

Dedication   v

Invitation   ix

Introduction   xv

Chapter One: Celebrate Where You Are In Christ   1

Chapter Two: Celebrate Being Accepted in Christ   17

Chapter Three: Celebrate Being Secure In Christ   33

Chapter Four: Celebrate Being Significant in Christ   51

Chapter Five: Celebrate Being an Ambassador
of Christ   65

Chapter Six: Celebrate Resting In Christ   79

Chapter Seven: Celebrate Following Christ   91

Chapter Eight: Celebrate Overcoming In Christ   109

Chapter Nine: Celebrate Your Inheritance
Through Christ   125

Chapter Ten: Celebrate Establishing a Godly
Heritage   141

Afterwards   157

About the Author   161

Invitation

Nehemiah 8:10 (NLT*) - ... Go and celebrate with a feast... and share gifts of food with people who have nothing prepared. This is a sacred day...Don't be sad, for the joy of the Lord is your strength!

This verse of the Bible is so special to the Mother in Love Series. It states the core vision of what our ministry is about and what the grace of God has allowed us to do as a family. We enjoy presenting women's conferences, speaking at churches, holding women's events, and teaching Bible studies. Celebrating the Good News of the love of Jesus is the banner and theme that we structure and build upon. When you come to a Mother in Love event, it truly does feel like a feast. One of the most meaningful parts of the day is when we fellowship over simple lunches, which allows us to share with all of the people who have gathered. We see where God is working in our lives and in theirs. We believe that this time spent together both physically and spiritually nourishes those who feel empty. It is our sincere prayer to share and introduce the individuals who attend to the source of the eternal Bread of Life on which their soul can forever feast.

It is so encouraging for everyone to be refreshed with the knowledge that God keeps His promises. That is a good reason to celebrate!

Any time that you set apart to spend with the Lord is sacred. Presently, I am at my kitchen table, sipping a cup of coffee, and writing this. I am living in the moment of what God has given me. If we saturate our hearts in the center of Christ as the power of our strength, we will find joy that casts out our sadness. This is a great concept for a devotional study. You are invited to come to the Lord's Table to feast on the bounty of His abundant grace. If you live each day with the mind-set of celebrating the gifts of the present, you will be drawn into the habit of creating a heavenly future. In other words, make God the focus of your celebration.

It is easier to do this when we recall life's journeys and milestones, knowing that God has been there supplying everything we need. We should celebrate occasions and people, but most of all, celebrate God. Deuteronomy 2:7 gives us a wonderful reminder: "The Lord your God has blessed you in everything you have done and has watched your every step...the Lord your God has been with you and provided for your every need so that you lack nothing."

To celebrate all the life changing gifts and experiences we have because of the great love of Jesus seems the perfect way to bring to a close the Mother in Love Series. During the process of attempting to bring out the principles of a heart centered in Christ, as was modeled for me, you have been welcomed to decide for yourself if you want to relate to the teachings available through the example of the life of Jesus. Each of us must come to believe for ourselves beyond any doubt that knowing and applying God's Word to our life is absolutely necessary if we have any hope of living in the moment and rejoicing in what God is doing for us today. The situations we face may not always look like something we want to celebrate, but, if we cultivate a relationship with Jesus, we know there is plenty to be glad about.

My mother-in-law loved to sing and she sang almost every time I was with her. It was the way she was so unashamed about joyfully singing to the Lord that caused me to tune into the words of her songs. Even now as I'm praying about what to share that would be a blessing, I can hear her voice and true to who she was, she is singing.

I remember the first few years after I first came into the family as a young bride. I didn't know many songs about Jesus or that He wanted to be my friend. The songs were always simple, which was good for me, but they impacted my life because of the power of the words. One example –says it all:

He has made me glad

He has made me glad

I will rejoice because He has made me glad

I have not thought about the words of that song nor heard them sung since the years that she has been called home to be with the Lord. But thinking about them now, those words were truly how my mother-in-law lived. Each of her days was celebrated by being in the presence of the Father, Son and Holy Spirit. This brought much happiness to her. These words may not be on the American Top 20 countdown list, but I am sure they were inspired to tell us something of the mighty God we have. Sometimes the world and people here will not fulfill our every need or stay with us when the hardships of life threaten to overwhelm us past our ability to handle them. Our God promises that, whatever we are going through, we can rejoice and be glad because of the constant assurance He will be there. His word says that He will never leave us or forsake us — and that is one of the many reasons that our heart can live with the beating praise of celebration, no matter what. Read these words for yourself and be encouraged that you have a forever friend. Deuteronomy 31:6 confidently states: "Be strong and courageous! Do not be afraid of them!

The Lord your God will go ahead of you. He will neither fail you, nor forsake you." Lift your head and know that there is no fear for those who trust in the favor of the Lord. As children of God, we are dearly loved, fiercely protected, and never alone.

Because of the way my mother-in-law celebrated her friendship with Jesus, I began to notice His importance in her life. She took every open opportunity to share with me exactly how God's love could transform any life to a renewed life. Eventually, I picked up on the words of the songs she sang. I wanted those messages in my life, too, so that I could teach them to my children. It was as my husband and I were starting our family, after the birth of our second child, that I decided that I wanted Jesus to be real in my life. I became a Christian because of the songs and the spiritual guidance of a woman who was not afraid to celebrate Jesus. She lived with a heart full of the pure and ripe fruit of the Spirit (Galatians 5:22-23). People are attracted to those who practice the behavior of living in the heavenly abundance that Jesus came to give. You can be sure that the more God dwells in us, the more we will look different to the world and to those around us. Jesus tells us in His own words what His purpose here on earth was. In John 10:10, He states, "My purpose is to give life in all its fullness."

With that said, ask the Holy Spirit to prepare your heart and to open your mind before we take a deeper look at God's stories and Scripture to discover why we can celebrate the life He has given us.

We do not have to wait for heaven to start claiming its victory and rejoice in its glory. Hope of eternal life can make us eternally happy because we can know that what we are presently going through one day will end and does not compare with what God has waiting. Together we can attempt to shake off the "stinking thinking" of negative living so we can free ourselves up to lighten up and live in the love of Jesus. Pattern your thoughts after Matthew 6:19-21 ....and let's get started. Remind yourself as often as needed that where your treasure is, there your heart and thoughts will be also. A life lived in celebration, starts in the thoughts and overflows into our actions. Will you commit to joyfully looking forward to sharing in God's glory? I am ready ... what are you waiting for?

The Biblical references made throughout this book are taken from the New Living Translation (NLT) version, unless specified otherwise.

Introduction

What does the word "celebration" mean to you? Do imagines immediately flash in your mind of loud gatherings, festive music, and gifts with a few party hats and streamers mixed in? For most of us, that is probably what a celebration looks like if we had to describe it. The common factor that a celebration seems to imply to just about everyone is the picture of a light hearted occasion filled with happiness and a joyful atmosphere. In this reflective study we are going to engage in possibly a new way of defining what a celebration is. Sometimes it is hard not to get distracted and think that its people, things, and the cheers of the world that will make us happy and make life meaningful.

Together we will take time and discover that a heart lived in daily celebration needs a Source which is able to meet our every need. It is the unending source of God's love through His Son which offers the greatest fulfillment we all want. The reason why a Christian can celebrate is because they have measured their love, acceptance, security, significance and value by what God has to say about His people. Are you in need of knowing how deep, how wide and how great the Father's love is for you? Do you think knowing how exceptional the God of the universe thinks you are would encourage you to celebrate the place you are right now in your life? Well, I can promise you that the party can begin! I can promise you that if we ask God to be our first guest, He will show up every time on time.

In this concluding study of the Mother in Love series, we will place the last piece of living a Christ-centered life along with all the others we have already built on. The stages we have completed so far are living in the power of the Holy Spirit (Book One – Hanging on the vine…), the blessings of going back and remembering the start of our relationship with Jesus (Book Two – Back to the Beginning…), the gift of praying to, thanking and praising our Heavenly Father (Book Three – Raise the Roof…) and learning how to use the tools provided for establishing a productive, Christian life through God's Word (Book Four–Work in Progress…)

Now we will turn our attention to what makes a celebration with a spiritual intention unique. It all begins with taking the time out of the ordinary to honor and observe something noble and important to us all, the wonders of eternity.

Whether we are leaping for joy before the Lord as King David expresses throughout the book of Psalms, or quietly reflecting on God's Word at the Lord's Supper as Jesus taught us, we need to frequently pause and remember what the gifts of God are. The end result of all celebration should be joy, the joy that comes from a filled and grateful heart. God has extended to us the ultimate reason to rejoice, because He has sent away for us to be rescued from the consequences that sin calls for (See Romans 6:20-23). Those who willingly and faithfully believe that, have the most to celebrate. What can be better than receiving love that can never be stripped away?

It appears the question we will seek to find clarity with is: Can we really live in a celebratory attitude despite what life seems to be throwing at us? I want to propose to you, through personal experiences, that even after the cake is gone and the last guest has departed from the party, the celebration can long continue. I can understand it may be hard to believe at the moment if all we are looking at is the shredded remains of streamers, the pieces of deflated balloons, and the mountain of a big mess to clean up. I do not want to discredit the severity of some of the daily difficulties we have to persevere with. Problems such as the economy, physical and mental health, conditions plaguing the world, global warming, and whatever else that can be named are never ending. Without a doubt, I am certain that you can add to the list which runs on and on.

As alarming as this all is, we have a choice where to focus our thoughts. In the middle of the storm, our hope can cling tightly to the source of Peace and find reason to be glad. Philippians 4:7 explains that this is true: "If you do this, (concentrate on what is good), you will experience God's peace, which is far more wonderful than the human mind can understand. His peace will guard your heart and minds as you live in Christ Jesus." If your desire is stirred to celebrate the things that God says are good, then I challenge you to read one verse down in Philippians to 4:8.

Would you like to be introduced to ideas that will allow you to do more than just make it through your days, but actually sense joy and find blessing in them? When you turn to Jesus as the only key to your happiness, you will be amazed at the way your life will be empowered to content, whatever the situation. If you are convinced that living in celebration will benefit the way you live your life, please join in the final study. Once our hearts and minds are open, our world is enlarged and wonderful experiences will be let in!

Before we delve into God's Word, I will mention that I have at the beginning of each book interweaved each concept of reflection with sharing my personal moments where mom shared them with me. It is with cherished memories that I recall one of the last of those moments I had with her in this life where she reflected the love of Jesus through her life's testimony.

Joy in the journey...

My mother-in-law's last lesson to me was just as impressive as her first examples of what unwavering faith looked like. She was the person I went to when I needed to see that this love for Jesus was real and that we could completely trust our lives to the One who gave us His and who created ours.

Mom had a way of keeping us girls connected to the Lord and grounded in His Word. We gathered for Bible studies and prayer meetings regularly. She took Titus 2:1 as her personal calling and motto – "Promote the kind of living that reflects right teaching." (This is the verse that describes our mission's aspiration.) The intention was always about striving to live the message of the Bible. Mom was an extraordinary representative of what a "Titus 2" woman was expected to accomplish. Verses 4 and 5 were the most valuable gifts she left for us as her daughters and daughters-in- law. One of the highest standards of Godly virtue in a woman is highlighted in this passage: "These older women must train the younger women to love their husbands, and their children, to live wisely and pure, to take care of their homes, to do good, and to be submissive to their husbands. Then they will not bring shame on the Word of God."

Mom believed in this deeply as the foundation of a strong home, and was convinced that if she could pass that on to us then her family would have the deep-seated roots of a Godly heritage for generations to come. As we read in chapters 2 & 3 of Genesis, God's intention for marriage and perfect plan for man, woman and their children was intimate closeness with Him.

So, with the same beliefs embedded in my heart, these studies have traced, through scripture principles, a families walk with the Lord as directed under His guidance.

Towards the end of mom's life her journey was not easy. But, what I remember the most is the joy she found in the middle of the unknown. When it was evident that she was not doing well and that something seriously wrong might be going on, we got together to pray over mom and ask for God's will in this situation we yet knew nothing about. It was strange to pull up to the house and not see mom in the window, sitting in her place at the kitchen table with her cup of coffee, waiting for us all to get there. I could tell immediately by the atmosphere that this night was going to be different. Most of the girls were already there and I instantly noticed that some of the women in the family who normally did not come to these occasions were there too. This set my mind wondering in directions I did not want it to go. None of us knew then that this evening was only the start of what would amount to six-month duration of the unknown needing to be faced.

Numerous things were different in the structure of what I was used to at our prayer meetings. One thing did remain the same, mom did not seem rattled. As I entered her bedroom, she was already in a chair with her robe on and had a blanket across her legs. Although it was comforting to see her holding her usual cup of coffee, this signaled another clue that difficult changes were coming because mom stayed dressed down to her shoes and socks until she was ready for bed.

But, I was greeted always with her warming smile and engaging eyes. Her eyes were as bright as they always had been, but I could see that she was tired. This time we were not only there to pray, but to hear the results of the doctor's visits. About eight of us spread across the bedroom finding places where we could. We were on the bed, on the floor, and in chairs waiting to hear what our next step was.

The best that we could be told was that the no one knew for sure at that moment what exactly the problem or problems were. It was the opinion of the doctor and the agreed upon decision that the tests needed to be done would require being admitted to the hospital. Mom's sister Nan and oldest daughter Betty would be the ones that would be staying with her and acting on her behalf as her advocate once more serious issues needed to be addressed. After processing the information, we got to the reason we were there: to pray.

My lesson this time did not come through what we were discussing or praying about, but, it happened when we were moving into the kitchen for coffee and cake. Everyone headed out and I stayed behind. I was overwhelmed at the possibility of how sick mom could be and I could not bear the thought of her not being here. As she stood up to make her way out of the room, I went over and hugged her and also told her how much I loved her. She meant the world to me and I needed her to know that. Since the opportunity presented itself for us to have a moment alone, I asked her if she was afraid. Her face lit up with a look of secure content. Her answer suggested that she had already thought about this.

Mom explained that, of course, she wanted everything to work out and be okay, but that if it did not, she would still be able to accept the outcome. "Being healed would be awesome," she said, "but I know God has me." It was more important to her that her children and grandchildren see God's work in whatever He was about to do. In that moment, that was her source of joy. She looked forward to celebrating the only thing that she could, the eternal victory that everyone in Christ can claim. Mom decided that her path was to continue to be faithful, and to go where Jesus would lead. The apostle Paul expressed similar feelings of faith. In Philippians 1:21-22 (Good News Translation) he says, "For what is life? To me, it is Christ. Death, then, will bring more. But if by continuing to live

I can do more worthwhile work, then I am not sure which I should choose."

The point is that when we trust God's outcome, we can celebrate where the journey will take us. I believe that was what Mom was saying to me that night. Fear was not an option because God promises to remove all our fear. For the next several months, we walked alongside mom in celebration. I witnessed through the hospital stays, treatments, and her physical discomfort, what it is to be joyful in the Lord. I promise you that it is not about liking the situation, but resting in the assurance that Jesus is there with us.

All the details of the private battle mom experienced with her health are not the focus; it was her endurance to commit herself to her Savior until the end that has inspired me to know that our God does not fail us. When mom knew in her heart that she had completed her journey here, we brought her home so that her last few days could be spent in prayer, singing and praising the Lord just as she had always done.

As we begin our final study; keep these words as an encouragement: (James 1:2-4) "My friends, consider yourself fortunate when all kinds of trails come your way, for you know that when your faith succeeds in facing such trials, the result is the ability to endure. Make sure that your endurance carries you all the way without failing, so that you may be perfect and complete, lacking nothing." That complete faith is what I witnessed through the legacy of a life centered on the perfection founded in a relationship with Jesus.

Format of Devotions

At the conclusion of each chapter, there is a section intended to draw you into God's Word, called <u>Questions For Your Spirit</u>. Here is where you will want to take time and let your heart connect with God. This is a good experience to have within a group environment or for your own personal reflection time. After you finish considering the questions, you can move on to the section entitled <u>Scripture to Celebrate</u>. This section offers you more scripture readings pertaining to the topic that was discussed. A helpful suggestion is to go further into the message and meditate on God's Word as you write out the verses that have been referenced.

The blank pages after the chapter entitled <u>What I Will Celebrate</u> are for you to record any additional thoughts or answers that you may want to remember.

Journaling is a way for us to look at our thoughts. It can be a great source of inspiration to write down the moments when the Holy Spirit is moving in your life. The insights that we receive are precious. Located in the very back of the book you will notice even more blank pages headed with <u>Moments to Rejoice</u>. Please capture anything that has been meaningful to you so that you can continue to grow deeper in the celebration of your relationship with Jesus.

Chapter One:

Celebrate Where You Are In Christ

Celebrate God's Word - You chart the path ahead of me and tell me where to stop and rest. Every moment you know where I am. – Psalm 139:3

"What is God's will for my life?" This is not an uncommon question for many Christians. Usually when we are walking a little out of step in our spiritual relationship we will begin to contemplate where our life is and what purpose it has, but, when our walk with God is close we are already in His will. God's will for those who claim His name does not change. We are expected to live aware that He is there. Sometimes we are so busy charting our own path and plotting our own course we might forget to consider that we are possibly already at the place God wants us, at least for now. More frequently than I'd like to admit, I wear a big "guilty" sign attesting to that. I get so caught up with self-inflicted thinking about needing to rush aimlessly around, feebly trying in myself, to do more and be more for God and those in my life.

I have a sense that it is my sole responsibility to take on the full weight of every situation, and I claim it whether it is mine or not. Are you familiar with any of this? With everything we do in a day, and since running through the day is such common behavior, does the thought of celebrating where we are at in the moment seem impossible? It has been my experience that when we avoid taking the time to stop, rest, and gain vision of our lives with Spiritual eyes, we can never fully know or appreciate where we truly are. Without "slowing your roll" (a favorite expression of one of my sister-in-laws), you tend to get tired and sloppy, which causes life to feel like you're living it on a hamster wheel. You can be certain that we are incapable of moving fast enough to escape the loving, watchful eye of God. As the verse says, "Every moment He knows where we are."

There is great temptation to measure the success of our lives by comparing the way things are now to the accomplishments we think we should have already achieved. Such comparison complicates the process of celebrating the place God has brought us to. God is not at all impressed by what we accumulate on Earth. He is not the least bit concerned with the prestige of our addresses or if we have gold name plates on high-rise office doors. Those are not the places where He finds us. We have a God of the heart who opens us up to search our souls and transform our thinking. When we find ourselves living at peace with where we are, it empowers us to pass on the things that God has given us. Once we realize Christ is working in us, we grasp that there is no better place to be. I believe we have been given the message of forgiving each other, loving each other, sharing what we have with each other, improving the lives of each other and telling everyone that God gives His love to everyone.

Think for a moment about the times you are most happy and content. If you are like me, it is when relationships are going well, health is good, the needs for food and clothes are met, bills are paid and the general flow of my home is without friction. Most of us can agree these are priceless gifts. When we are controlled by a Spiritual focus instead of money-controlled indulgence, what is really important becomes clearer and we have reason to celebrate. Please do not hear me wrong. Money is in no way evil, but the love of money gives deep roots to distorting the joy we feel towards our lives. (Reference 1 Timothy 6:6-10) The point about celebrating where we are in Christ is about the day we are ushered into eternity to meet Him. Will our home, car, job or even our wardrobe matter? From what I know about Jesus, my educated guess? No. The real issues of the soul will be His only interest. Have we been faithful in our faith? Have we loved our neighbors more than ourselves? Do we know God in a special way? If those are questions that can be answered with a yes, then the celebration begins right here today. I can assure you that we can rejoice now in the things that we have to look forward to in heaven. God has wonderful plans He wants to accomplish through us and marvelous promises He wants to give us. 1 Corinthians 14:1 says that if we want to experience joy and a life of righteousness which will never run dry, then we must let love be our highest goal. No one has celebrated a life lived in Christ by keeping it to themselves.

The writer Oswald Chambers understood the Christian faith. He knew the intention and devotion it took to live it, but, he also knew how to explain it pointedly through his writings. In the book *My Utmost for His Highest*, Chambers expresses his view on why joy can only abound in maintaining a right relationship with Jesus. The excerpt that I share from his book focuses on the words taken from the Scripture passage, John 15:11. Here we find Jesus encouraging His disciples with these words, "I have told you this so that you will be filled with my joy. Yes, your joy will over flow.

This is how Chambers interprets what Jesus is saying: "The first thing that will hinder this joy is the captious irritation of thinking out circumstances. The cares of this world, said Jesus, will choke God's Word. Before we know where we are, we are caught up in the show of things. All that God has done for us will be a mere threshold; He wants to get us to the place where we can be His witnesses and proclaim who Jesus is. Be rightly related to God, find your joy there, and out of you will flow rivers of living water. Be a center for Jesus Christ to pour living water through. Stop being self-conscious, stop being a sanctified prig, and live the life hid with Christ. The life that is rightly related to God is as natural as breathing wherever it goes. The lives that have been of most blessing to you are those who were unconscious of it."

Reading that portion revealed to me that having the correct perception of where we are in our walk with Jesus is the essential key if we are to unlock the door to celebrating the life we have been given and the season of it we currently experience. We are taught over and over again in God's word that it is never the actual situation we are in that brings happiness to our lives, but the peace of having God with us while we are there. Let's take a closer look at one person who could have been a little upset with where life had taken her, but chose to remain close to the God she knew was always faithful as she looked forward to the promised Messiah who would save her people.

Esther's story: The Queen of Persia.

Esther is one of only two books in the Bible named after women. Her story is written out and waits to be used as a testimony that God can do extraordinary things through the ordinary events of our lives. As her story opens, we are introduced to an ordinary Jewish orphan being raised by her cousin, Mordecai. But even before Esther is aware of her destiny, God has been preparing it.

In the third year of his reign, King Xerxes gave an exquisite banquet for his highest officials, princes and noblemen of the empire he ruled. The celebration lasted six months, a tremendous display of the great wealth of the land. When this was over, another feast ordered by the king began. At the same time, his wife, Queen Vashti, was hosting a banquet of the same caliber for the women who belonged to the royal palace. There was no expense spared, with the only restriction being not to take more than you wanted.

It was on the seventh day of the second celebration that the party atmosphere took a turn. While drunk with wine, the people began pressuring King Xerxes to call for his queen. She was a very beautiful woman and they wanted her to appear beside the king wearing the royal crown. This background information sets the scene for the role Esther was chosen to fill, ushered in by the King's banquet. Queen Vashti was summoned, but refused to appear. Her answer infuriated the king and brought down his wrath upon her. It was decided that she would be forever banished from the land. The palace was now without a queen.

Even though Jesus had not yet come to earth during the time of Esther, her people lived in expectation of the One to be sent by God to save them from their oppression. They could still celebrate Christ without actually knowing His name. What the Jews did know was that God had promised freedom and that the One who was coming would be employed as the great Deliverer. This need for deliverance has been continuous throughout human history, since creation and the fall of man, due to the evidence of ever-growing sinfulness keeping us separated from God. The prophet Isaiah spoke to the Lord's people and gave them His words about the coming suffering servant to be sent (Isaiah 52 & 53). This is one of the many passages in Scripture pointing to Jesus as the foretold Messiah. Some of this background knowledge may be helpful because although the Jewish people lived amongst many trials, the hope of being rescued from their situation certainly gave them hope for a future that could be celebrated in advance.

As we recall in Esther's story, the palace was without a queen. It was proposed that the position be filled by a young beautiful woman, chosen by the king from among several young women throughout the land, who were forcibly taken. It would the one who pleased the king the most who would be adorned with the crown and become Queen of Persia. The king was amenable to this idea, and the orders were carried out.

In the fortress of Susa, where many Jews took refuge after the exile from Jerusalem, we meet Mordecai and the lovely Hadassah, known to us as Esther. After the brutal killing of her parents, Mordecai raised her as his own daughter. With palace officials snatching away young girls, Mordecai warned Hadassah of the danger of using her Jewish name. He begged her to use Esther for her own protection, if she were to be taken. Her nationality and family background were to be kept secret at all cost. Inevitably, Esther ended up in the king's harem. Her life was uprooted for a second time.

I can imagine the questions playing around in Esther's mind, such as, "How did I get here?" "Why is this happening to me?" "This is not where I want to be." "Haven't I been through enough?" "How am I ever going to get out of this?" "What do I do next?" I also believe that at this point, she was not looking forward to the thought of being brought before the King for his approval. She probably would want to be as far away as possible from where she was. We could all relate somehow to the story of Esther. In just an instant, our lives can change and we find ourselves in the midst of circumstances beyond our control and capability to handle it.

It is the perspective we choose to live in that will determine whether we retreat in self-defeating attitudes or use our abilities to turn a difficult situation into one that serves God and others. Stopping to realize the impact of our reactions often changes the problem, weakness, sorrow, or struggle we are experiencing into wonderful moments that can be used in the place God has brought us to for His purpose. It is not always going to be the situation that makes us happy, but rather celebrating the victory we have, as God is in control of every situation. Esther did in fact find favor with the king and was chosen to be his queen, an occasion that began another celebration in honor of the newly-crowned queen.

But trouble soon started. The extinction of the Jewish people was being plotted by an evil-hearted palace official. Word of this uprising reached the queen and the conspirator was someone she knew. With the honeymoon barely over, the happy bride faced despair once again, just as life was looking good and going her way, or so it seemed. The king deeply loved Esther, but what would he do once he found out that the Jewish people he would be asked to do away with were also her people? Esther knew she must make a request of the king. Fear arose inside her as she wondered how she could possibly save an entire race of people. It was well known that anyone who appeared before the king uninvited would be put to certain death. Even the queen could not walk into his presence, rather she must be summoned. Talk about a dilemma! She could possibly lose her life or sentence her people to execution.

This was definitely a "what do I do" moment? Would this be a time to be thinking about celebrating? For Esther, it seemed liked the perfect time. Let's read what she decided to do straight from God's Word. Turn your Bible to Esther 5:1-7.

Three days later, Esther put on her royal robes and entered the inner court of the palace, directly across from the king's hall. The king was sitting on his royal throne, facing the entrance. When he saw Queen Esther standing in the inner court, he welcomed her, holding out his gold scepter to her. (This was a symbol that her presence was accepted – italics mine) So Esther approached and touched its tip. Then the king asked her, "What do you want, Queen Esther? What is your request? I will give it to you, even if it is half the kingdom." Esther replied. "If it pleases Your Majesty, let the king and Haman come today to a banquet I have prepared for the king." The king turned to his attendants and said, "Tell Haman to come quickly to a banquet, as Esther has requested." So the king and Haman attended Esther's banquet. While they were drinking wine, the king said to Esther, "Now tell me what you really want. What is your request? I will give it to you even if it is half the kingdom." Esther replied, "This is my request and deepest wish. If Your Majesty is pleased with me and wants to grant my request, please come with Haman tomorrow to the banquet I will prepare for you. Then tomorrow I will explain what this is all about."

Esther's life was spared by the king and for the time being, she was safe. She went before the king humbly and with great respect for his authority. Esther not only placed herself before the king's authority, but honored him with a celebration to show that she knew the high place he held. Considering his position, he was the only one capable of granting the request she was about to make. What is our method when life threatens us with danger, discomfort, or disappointment? Do we approach God like that? Instead of complaining or fretting about what is going on, do we ever consider spending some time celebrating who He is, how high above us He is, or how awesome He is? Or, do we out of habit give God the list of what is not right, and expect Him to change our circumstances? These are such challenging topics to think about.

During the banquet the next day, Esther courageously responded with her request to the king when asked. Everything that had brought Esther to the palace began to unfold; God had her stationed exactly where He wanted her for this purpose. When asked what she wanted, she replied, "If Your Majesty is pleased with me and wants to grant my request, my petition is that my life and the lives of my people will be spared. For my people and I have been sold to those who would kill, slaughter, and annihilate us. If we had only been sold as slaves, I could remain quiet, for that would have been a matter too trivial to warrant disturbing the king" (Esther 7:3-4).

The king immediately took action and granted her request. Those who thought their schemes had succeeded were quickly and publicly executed. Following this, a decree to help the Jews went out to all of the princes, governors, and local provincial officials from India to Ethiopia. The Jews in every city were given the authority to unite in order to defend their lives. None of this would have happened if Hadassah, the orphaned girl, did not believe that God would deliver His people. Queen Esther did receive her happily ever after, not because things went well all the time, but because she had a king who loved her and a Heavenly Father she knew was big enough to supply daily what she needed. Celebrations will not happen by sitting still; your life will not find joy if you do not choose to get it. Esther did not wait for God's will to be accomplished by standing on the sidelines. She got involved by being determined to contribute to her destiny and to that of her people. Because of her participation, she enjoyed the result of sharing in God's purpose.

To get the full effect of this story, I challenge you to read it for yourself in its entirety. We briefly scanned over the highlights to conclude a point. After sharing in Esther's life, have you looked into yours? Let's evaluate where we are right now. Are you celebrating? I can promise you that if we apply some of the same principles we just read about, there will be more reasons than we are aware of to be at peace with what God has given us. Have confidence that God is in control every second of your life and you are not beyond His reach. He knows exactly where you are. In closing, consider this: perhaps God has brought you into your situation "for such a time as this." Don't miss it, walk with spirit filled eyes, and find the celebration that your life was meant to be.

Questions For Your Spirit

- How do you feel about where you are in your life? Do you measure your life against the standards of society which you strive to attain? Do circumstances dictate whether or not you experience joy and consider yourself happy?

- Celebration is viewed as something that happens to commemorate only good things. When we are not feeling in the party mood, we think there is no reason to celebrate. Consider this thought: A Christian celebration should be to worship and to thank God because He loves us, because of His blessings to us and because of the eternal gift of salvation through Jesus waiting for all of us. Does that statement change the definition of celebration for you? Would you agree that it is a practice needed every day? If yes, why would that attitude be helpful?

- We have established that a celebratory outlook is strengthened by our relationship with God and the perspective of our thinking regarding each situation we encounter. Read Psalm 69:32-33. What kind of hope does this verse offer? What are the reasons we have to celebrate the present moment we are in?

- As we think about the story of Esther that was shared and your Bible reading of the details of her story, what are the things most relevant to you? Can you relate to her attitude of hope in some difficult trials? What other things about her character can you detect? In what ways has this example been an encouragement to you so that you can find joy and celebrate the purpose your life is for?

- Proverbs 31 echo's Esther's life as the passage exemplifies how a virtuous woman lives, especially from verse ten on. The lines that I believe deserve to be mediated on are verses 30-31.Charm is deceptive, and beauty does not last; but a woman who fears the Lord will be greatly praised. Reward her for all she has done. Let her deeds publicly declare her praise.

Reflect on that proverb and the implication of those sentences. Make it your prayer that your heart would be open to see the life God gave you as one to celebrate. Write out whatever the Spirit reveals to you. Do you live as a woman seeking the heart of the King? What is inspiring to you from this verse?

Scripture to Celebrate

2 Corinthians 1:3-4, Romans 8:28, 1 John 2:3, 2 Thessalonians 2:16-17, Isaiah (40:31 & 26:3), Luke 14:33

1Corinthians 15:54-58, Psalm 121:8, Ecclesiastes 5:19-20, Matthew 5:3, Jeremiah 17:7, Hebrews 13:5

What I Will Celebrate

What I Will Celebrate

Chapter Two:

Celebrate Being Accepted in Christ

Celebrate God's Word – You love Him, although you have not seen Him, and you believe in Him, although you do not now see Him. So you rejoice with a great and glorious joy which words cannot express, because you are receiving the salvation of your souls, which is the purpose of your life in Him. 1 Peter 1:8-9 (Good News Version)

The words from this verse were penned by the Apostle Peter, who walked with Jesus and bore witness to His suffering. It was the first of his two letters. Peter's objective throughout the entire letter was to encourage readers who faced persecution and suffering. He reminded the people constantly of the Good News about Jesus whose death, resurrection, and promised coming gave them hope. The hope of knowing that they were accepted by the sacrifice of Jesus allowed them to endure their testing. Mixed together with Peter's words of encouragement, he extended an urgent plea to Christians to live as people who belong to

Christ. He wanted to emphasize that being God's people should significantly affect our character. In other words, the message was and is to live a life celebrating the truth that we are accepted into a new unbroken relationship with God through Christ, who provided the way for our sins to be forgiven. This is known as salvation.

Being saved means freedom from the power of sin and victory over bad habits so that you can live a new life. Jesus offers us all a second chance at life. His acceptance gives us the opportunity to experience a spiritual rebirth into a regenerated life of the Spirit. Once we choose to accept God's Son, God accepts us forever. How amazing.

Unger's Bible Dictionary defines the word accepted as "to take pleasure in"; "to receive with hospitality"; "to receive with pleasure and kindness"; "a time of favor or a favorable opportunity". Let's consider this definition as our starting point. It highlights again why those who have accepted salvation through Jesus have reason to celebrate and to live their earthy life in the hope of the eternal life to come. Read those important words again and say them out loud as you do; pleasure, hospitality, kindness and favor. For me, it puts a fresh perspective on the acceptance we find in the relationship with God. Do you experience being treated that way? Those types of actions and encounters convey a positive message that we are of value to another person do they not? God also, through His Word and evidence of His work all around us, extends that same message. But, the only way for us to receive that message is to be open and receptive to it. We feel His love and acceptance when we spend time with Him and choose to listen to the quiet way that God speaks in our lives. Listening to God allows Him to care for us as He would like. It sound easy enough, but how is it that we are going to hear God? Psalm 46:10 tells us that our directions are to be silent, and know that He is God. Doing this enables us to understand who God is.

How comforting is it to know that once God accepts us, He will never reject us? In Romans 8:38, the Apostle Paul says, "I am convinced that nothing can ever separate us from the love of God." These are important words for those who may have experienced the other side of acceptance—rejection. The pain of rejection can sometimes be great, and it has the potential effect of causing emotional separation in the relationships we engage in. The consequences brought by the feeling of being discarded, unwanted, or defective are devastating. The negative blow of rejection definitely affects how we find ourselves joy and what outlook on celebration we can have. Though others may reject us, what is only important is this—that nothing on earth or below has the power to ever separate us from God's love or snatch us out of the palm of His protective hand. Living in this belief is the only cure for recovering from the emptiness of rejection. We need to daily invite and be filled up with the Holy Spirit of God if we want to enjoy our lives. I suggest that you should not try to deal with rejection all by yourself but bring every concern to God. The concept here is that when you turn to God, you will receive the Holy Spirit (Acts 2:38) because God is always calling us back to Him (Jeremiah 3:22). I Peter 5:7 explains the way to move away from the destructive lies of rejection and into a life of acceptance: "Give all your worries and cares to God, for He cares about what happens to you." It stands to reason then that if we do not value something as special, we are not likely to care what happens to it. Throughout the Bible, God cannot say enough about how much His love is for us, and how treasured we are to Him. Every time I contemplate this, it erases any doubt that the acceptance I need comes from anywhere else but from the Father because the Lord accepts all those who come to Him by faith.

I think that our understanding is deepening of how important the human need for acceptance is. When that basic need remains unmet, our feelings of self-worth are threatened. How can we hope to live confidently when we are struggling with issues of neglect, abandonment, and self-esteem? These thoughts now convey the messages of "I am worthless," "Something has to be wrong with me," and "No one wants me anyway." Are you beginning to see how having the wrong definition of acceptance can mess with your whole perception of yourself? It is dangerous ground, I can promise you, when we do not know what God thinks about us. Letting the world define us by its standards holds us captive in negativity when we cannot seem to measure up. The way to keep a healthy check on ourselves is not to cling to ungodly distractions. Don't risk your walk with God by being trapped by these negative standards, but set your mind on moving towards the love of God knowing that you are totally accepted—never abandoned, rejected or left alone.

Acceptance Found at the Well:

The story is of an unnamed woman. She went to the well simply to get water. In her mind, there was nothing special about her or about this day. What appeared to be a chance encounter with a stranger instantly changed her life forever. The empty bucket that she carried was about to be filled with something she never expected to be given or had experienced before. Come and listen closely to what may be one of the most important conversations this lady has ever had. Listen as we hear the words of Jesus tell her "everything she'd ever done." Within just a few moments of this brief interaction, a life goes from knowing only rejection to being introduced to the source of abundant acceptance.

Scripture invites us in to that private exchange between Jesus and the Samaritan woman as they met at the well. John 4:4-42 describes the whole scene as it walks us through the entire event. Jesus had His work cut out for Him long before He even stopped to rest and get something to drink in the region of Samaria. The woman coming up the path was carrying more than a bucket or clay jar on her shoulders; she was carrying the heavy weight and burdens of her life, issues she had held on to for years, unaware that she was being strangled by the hold her lifestyle had on her.

Not being accepted as anything important was nothing new. After all, she was a woman and a Samaritan on top of that. These were two strikes, so to speak, already against her. In those times there wasn't anything worse you could be. It is not a secret that women were not regarded in the same way as they are today. At the time in which this story was happening, women were valued even less than animals. Besides that, the Jewish people deeply despised the Samaritan people. So our friend already had the baggage of rejection associated with her from birth.

Samaritans were hated because they were a mixed race with a pagan core; they were seen to be unlike the Jewish people, who considered themselves the purest of the races both in blood line and nobility. Because Jesus was Jewish, He could have very easily passed by this city because it was deemed unclean and a place His people did not associate with. Giving this very sparse explanation of the background of the two people groups represented here, will help in our understanding of the woman's reaction when she meets Jesus as we continue in the story a little further.

Why is it that Jesus went out of His way and off the route He was traveling to become involved for a moment in the life of this lady He should have had nothing to do with? As we begin to read, follow along in your Bible. In the book of John (Chapter 4) Jesus and His disciples were leaving Judea and returning to Galilee. Much to His companions' displeasure Jesus wanted to take the longer route going through, as we mentioned, the forbidden land of Samaria. Exhausted from the demands of travelling by foot, Jesus decides it is time to stop for a while. John 4:5-6 tells us that eventually He came to the Samaritan village of Sychar. This place is significant because it is the parcel of land that Jacob gave to his son, Joseph. Jacob's well was also there; so about noontime Jesus wearily sits down beside it. He is alone because the disciples went into the village to buy some food (John 4:8). I can picture Jesus leaning against the well deep in His own thoughts, enjoying the solitude and break. He notices another tired figure walking towards Him. Still too far in the distance to tell who it is, Jesus waits until the shadow of a woman becomes clear. Within a few more short feet, the woman approaching the well would never be the same again.

It seemed strange for her to be coming to the well this late; the woman of the village normally drew the water they needed very early in the morning. Could it be that this woman was attempting to avoid the stares and snide comments of the others who had already been there? Why else would she be alone and making the trip at this hour of the day? Based on the information we have so far, we can merely speculate that the person Jesus saw walking towards Him at the well in the heat of the day showed no evidence of thinking there was anything worth celebrating about her life. She was used to being not being accepted in any social circle. All she ever knew so far was the pain of being shunned and treated as the outcast of the town. How would she react to Jesus? This situation was a cultural taboo from the start. First of all, a man was talking to a woman. Second, a Jewish man was talking to a Samaritan woman. Third, anything that a Samaritan had was unclean and was not to be taken. A Jewish person was to ensure he was ceremonially clean at all times. Doing what He usually does, Jesus goes forward and ignores everything man has ordained for the greater purpose of reaching out for someone's heart. As we read John 4:7, the first thing Jesus says to her is, "Please give me a drink."

John 4:9 is where their dialogue begins. This is perhaps one of the rare occasions when someone has wanted to accept something from her. Her response to what was going on, as we can well imagine, was that of surprise.

She said to Jesus, "You are a Jew and I am a Samaritan woman."

"Why are you asking me for a drink?" Some of the other thoughts playing in her mind might have even been, "If this man knew what I have done and where I have been, he surely would not be asking me for a drink." Her misconception that she was worthless and unwanted was about to be replaced with the truth. The man in front of her does indeed already know everything, and he does not hesitate to share that He is ready to give her everything her thirsty heart has ever desired.

Jesus replies, "If you only knew the gift God has for you and who I am, you would ask me, and I would give you living water" (John 4:10). With that statement, the shame of her past no longer matters. What takes its place is the brightness of a new future. Jesus did prove that He knew the woman, and He accepts her anyway. In verse 17, He goes on to tell her about her life. There is so much to this story, and there is no way to uncover all the richness of its meaning in this short rendition. But the point that is our focus is celebrating being accepted in Christ. Living water is flowing and fresh; it is constantly being refreshed. It does not have time to stand still or get stagnant; it is the best water you can offer someone. Would Jesus, in offering you the best He has, not make you feel really special and accepted as someone important to Him? Would you not have something to truly celebrate, if the Son of God wanted to fill your empty bucket with this? If we rush to the living water, which is the love God pours out on us, we will always have a place to find acceptance.

The world offers us temporary moments when we feel good, but feelings can quickly change. Listen to what Jesus says about His friendship, "People soon become thirsty again after drinking this water (living the way other people see us – explanation mine). But the water I give them takes away thirst altogether (finding acceptance in Christ – explanation mine). It becomes a perpetual spring within them, giving them eternal life" (John 4:13).

From what we can understand of this story, human relationships have disappointed this woman. God created our relationships to be good and satisfying, but they are never enough. Only the love of God in Christ is an inexhaustible fountain of love, joy, and peace that radiates into our lives as a celebration because the deepest needs of our soul have been met. After meeting Jesus in such a transparent way, the result for her is shown in her reply: "Please, sir, give me some of that water! Then I'll never be thirsty again, and I won't have to come here to haul water" (John 4:15). In essence she said, if you will be the source that keeps my life full, I will never have to fill my bucket with the burdens the world wants to lay upon me, because you will always love me. We can read in John 4:28 how the story concludes—with a restored person running boldly and confidently off to tell everyone she knows about what had just happened. She left her bucket at the well, cast at the feet of the One who welcomed her to take part in what He offered.

"Come!" she beckoned, "Come and meet a man who told me everything I ever did! Can this be the Messiah?" (John 4:29) It was evident to the whole village that her encounter was life-changing.

Because of the things the woman was saying, many Samaritans believed in Jesus. They went out to find Him so that they too could hear His message; and because they heard Him, they believed. It was only after Jesus spoke the same words to the crowd that they said to the woman, "Now we believe because we have heard Him ourselves, not just because of what you told us. He is indeed the Savior of the world" (Referenced from John 4:39-42).

This caused me wonder…what is Jesus waiting to say to each of us? Are you ready to trade in rejection, to celebrate the deep love of acceptance?

Questions For Your Spirit

- We used the woman at the well as our story illustration. Have you had a "well" experience with Jesus? Write out what it was like. Are there any similarities with the story in your account? You can keep this private, or can share it to encourage others.

- Meditate on the verses from Psalm 139:17-18. Write out your thoughts and what they say to you. Are these words helpful in defining how beautifully we are accepted in the eyes of God? Do you agree that this is something to celebrate? Begin your day by seeking God and you will find that He is already there.

"How precious are your thoughts about me, O God! They are innumerable! I can't even count them; they outnumber the grains of sand! And when I wake in the morning you are still with me."

- Jesus encourages us to locate the source of our acceptance. Read these Bible verses and record your thoughts: 1 John 3:1, Jeremiah 17:7, and Psalm 118:8. What is the source of your acceptance? As an extra challenge, write the verse out as you read it.

- On what do you depend for your feelings of worth? Read Matthew 10:29-31. What is revealed to you there about the thoughts of a loving God toward us? Are there any Scriptures special to you which point out that we are beyond price to Jesus? Record them to share or just reflect upon.

- Considering what we have researched through the Scriptures, and the personal exploration of our own hearts, do you feel worthy of this kind of acceptance? Do you celebrate the knowledge that Jesus already knows everything about you and without shame accepts you anyway, calling you His? After this study do you have a different definition of and attitude regarding acceptance? Before you answer the questions, think about this passage; see if it helps stir new thoughts. Prayerfully write what you are feeling.

Psalm 92:2 & 4-5

It is good to proclaim your unfailing love in the morning, your faithfulness in the evening. You thrill me, Lord, with all you have done for me! I will sing for joy because of what you have done. O Lord, what great miracles you do! And how deep are your thoughts.

Scripture to Celebrate

Psalm 94:14, 1 Peter 4:9-10, Revelation 21:4, Hebrews 1:13-14, Nahum 1:7, Malachi 4:2

Genesis 1:27-31, Joshua 10:14, Matthew 20:28, Mark 10:37-39, Acts 11:16-18, Exodus 26:12

What I Will Celebrate

What I Will Celebrate

Chapter Three:

Celebrate Being Secure In Christ

Celebrate God's Word – ... He set my feet on solid ground and steadied me as I walked along. Psalm 40:1-2

I want to state from the onset of this chapter what the central idea is for us. The point will be that when we build our lives on God's truth we have a solid foundation that will not crack under the world's pressure. With so much instability in the world and such rapid changes thrown at us in our lives, we need to hold on to the security of our faith in Christ. Faith is the crucial component in trusting God as our source of lasting security, for He is changeless. Through consistent and devoted prayer, we can sustain the security of God's supernatural peace. (Philippians 4:6-7)

If you think about it a moment, we invest a lot of time in planning for our security. Many of us have retirement portfolios to prepare for our financial security, and some people use home security systems to ensure the protection of their loved ones and property. These precautions are often taken because we feel threatened by the unpredictable nature of the world in which we live. Financial security, personal security, job security, relational security, and even the security of our nation are real issues for us. We care about those things so much because they relate to the greater dynamic of our need to feel safe. It is very unsettling to feel insecure. I believe that is why such intentional measures are taken to avoid being unprotected or vulnerable. Yet, as much as we attempt to plan for every unseen contingency that may happen, how much time do we spend making sure that our Spiritual lives are also guarded? Do you ever wonder if you are really protected? Even that question, I am sure, has already made some of us begin to feel a little unsecure.

To understand more fully the concept of security as it relates to celebrating the marvelous wonders we have in Christ, we must first recognize who we are – eternal beings wrapped up in a mortal, fleshly body. This simply means that even though we are contained in an earthy container, our bodies, there is inside in each one of us, a soul, which will go on to live forever. Yes, God is concerned about the safety and well-being our physical bodies. He was the one who crafted the blueprint and designed our earthy forms, and we probably had experienced His hand of protection more often than we ever realize. The soul is the being placed deep inside us that after we confess our faith in Jesus, the Holy Spirit will come to live in it. You can feel secure in knowing that even though God is concerned about our bodies, He is much more emphatically concerned about what happens to our souls. It is so important and life-changing to grasp that our bodies here on earth will eventually wear out, but our faith in Jesus gives our soul a safe passage to our eternal homes. He is the security and protection guarding and keeping for us that which is eternal — our souls. II Timothy 1:2 says, "...for I know the one whom I trust, and I am sure that He is able to guard what I have entrusted to Him until the day of His return." Are you secure enough in knowing who Jesus is to make that same statement? It is my sincere prayer that if you cannot make that statement right now, you will soon.

We most often will experience a secure feeling in Christ when we are following Him closely. The one example that comes to mind of this kind of closeness is that of a parent and child. Our greatest concern is in keeping our children safe and giving them a secure feeling that nothing is going to happen to them. This is done through the daily activities and interactions we have with them. When we go outside with our little ones, we hold their hand to make sure that they are securely in our reach. It is an unspoken promise that nothing without our knowledge will get close to them. You have possibly heard this phrase, "If they want to get to you; they will have to get through me first." In this special verse from John 10:14-16; we find Jesus saying the same thing as He was speaking with a crowd of people. Let these words bring you the security of knowing that Jesus wants you and I to follow Him and will guide us with safety wherever we go as children of God. "I am the Good Shepherd; I know my own sheep, and they know me, just as my Father knows me and I know the Father. And I lay down my life for the sheep. I have other sheep, too, that are not in this sheepfold. I must bring them also, and they will listen to my voice; and there will be one flock with one Shepherd."

Discernment and extreme caution must always be used to monitor our emotions. If it becomes a choice to live in the insecurity and dark suspicion that things could not get better but only worse, then we are pushing out any hope of celebrating what happens when we fix our eyes on Jesus. Being constantly shaken with negative feelings will cause insecurity to creep in and have us questioning every area of our lives. Trouble with feelings of security, I believe, will sooner or later open a door to hopelessness. Whenever we see the future with more clouds, frustrations, pain, sorrow, and problems, we invite in that spirit of hopeless, which is all too willing to infect our being. If we truly see life this way, we will stay in that rut of trouble: pain, problems and darkness.

But, the incredibly good news for us is there is another side to all that. At the heart and center of our souls is Jesus, who holds the hope of a "better way". To walk with Jesus brings the joy of living in celebration into our lives. If we come to Him, we will find out that His love is secure and more trustworthy than anything we could ever count on. Do you believe that living in perfect heaven is better than sinful earth? Do you believe that it is better to be forgiven than to be condemned? If you do, then you are secure for eternity my friends. Remember this. Jesus Christ, as the Son of God, is far superior to all things and all religions. Faith in Him alone is sufficient for a secure Christian life.

Are you tired of feeling insecure and letting the circumstances of the day dictate your emotional stability? If you want to move from fed-up to freed-up and anchor your security on the solid ground of Jesus, then be challenged to change. There are two ways to start. Number one is that we must know the Savior of Israel before anything will change in our lives. The way to becoming secure is to be confident in where our security comes from. Isaiah 43:1 pronounces... "But now, O Israel (place your name there to make this promise yours), the Lord who created you says, Do not be afraid, for I have ransomed you. I have called you by name; you are mine." Number two is that you have to set your mind on the course you want to take and do not detour. Picture this example: you are navigating in strange waters or maybe tracking through dangerous wilderness. You haven't any idea what is in front of you, but you know you must stay on the path. In which direction should you go? Would you feel more secure if there were a competent navigator along on this adventure with you? There is no need to answer; of course, you would. Listen, I won't try to trick you into believing it is easy out there. As we maneuver our way through spiritual territory, we will become frightened. New territory will tend to make us feel a little insecure and unsure; especially if we think that it is only filled with trouble. That is why trusting the one who is navigating is important, if we hope to make it out of our predicament. We must be fully confident that we have the support of the Lord God and have total faith that He knows the way! But you do not have to take my word for it. Hear for yourself: "When you walk through deep waters and great trouble, I will be with you. When you go through rivers of difficulty, you will not drown! When you walk through the fire of oppression, you will not be burned up; the flames will not consume you. For I am the Lord, your God, the Holy One of Israel, your Savior" (Isaiah 43:2-3a).

Is your security level rising? I think it should be. Now that we have established a point at which strong, secure feelings start, let's see if we can get out there and just live it! Just start walking; you know where to go.

Personal Story of Being Secure in Christ: (Letting your children grow and slowly go!)

Recently my husband and I discovered how your feeling of security can be tested at any time whether you are ready or not! The day was finally here; we took our son, our oldest child, our baby boy (but as any mother knows it's really "my" baby boy) and left him at college. Your head knows it's the right thing to do. Telling it to your heart is another issue all together. As I looked at this handsome, capable, 6-foot 2-inch young man standing before me, I was amazed at how fast 18 years went. My mind quickly scanned all the things that God had done in our lives over those past years to bring us here. I took my husband's hand to walk around the campus because it was time to let go of our son's hand. Our son was already in his dorm with his roommate, so we decided to stroll around; alone. Our conversation consisted mostly of memories on a day such as this and if we (okay, mostly me...I will give my husband this one) were up for the challenge of letting him go? It felt like we had been doing a lot of 'letting go' over the past summer. Not only did we have to let our son begin to spread his wings and begin his own flight pattern, Tom and I watched as our oldest daughter got her driver's license and sped into her junior year of high school. Our little girl was now part of the masses on the road. To add to the layers of icing being heaped upon the cake, the one who shares my birthday, the baby of my babies who just last year thought boys were yucky is now wearing make-up, straightening her hair and wearing nice clothes to school so they will now notice her.

Now I must say, YUCK! How can she be in eighth grade and thirteen already? Really? Someone please stop this ride; I want off! I want to go back about five years ago when Friday night was pizza and movie night. Not take-me-to-the-mall-so-I-can-hang-out-with-my-friend's night! What happened to mom and dad being great and the center of the universe? I turned around for one second and they go and grow up on me? Is it just me or can you tell that I am struggling here with feeling insecure with the whole idea that my family is growing up and moving on? This is where Tom and I are. We are in a new season of life with each other and with our three children.

What I see in my mind when I hear the word security is the image of an anchor. I picture a massive rock with a thick unbreakable rope that I can tie myself to. Once I am anchored to that rock, I know nothing can move me. And it works great at first, but I notice that if we do not keep a close eye on the knot we tied, it has the potential to loosen and begin to unravel. That is describing how I am feeling right about now. My knot seems to be fraying ever so slightly with each new change occurring in our household. It feels like the security I had known since the children were born is now slipping away and I need to feel anchored again to something. Meeting their every need, teaching them, playing with them, giving them values and keeping them protected is what we have always done. In that capacity of being parents, those particular roles are slowing starting to wind down, especially in the life our son.

These past three months or so, these types of conversations have been all-consuming ones in our marriage; at least on my end. God bless my husband, he really can be the sweetest thing. He does not interrupt me during conversations, allowing me to ramble on like a mother hen worried about her chicks and not having them all closely under her wings any more. This, I am sorry, is pretty scary stuff for me and has taken a lot of getting use too. (No, I am not there yet, but, continuing to working on it.) During the course of one of our recent "conversations", Tom reminded me that our anchor is God's Word and that God gave us a promise that we can be secure in Jesus right in the middle of everything that is going on in our lives. Proverbs 22:6 has been the secure promise we have been building on for the 18 years we have been parents: Teach your children to choose the right path, and when they are older, they will remain upon it. This has been the one thing we strove to do more than anything else for our children. I really don't think I was letting go of the security of that particular promise so much as not wanting to face the reality that it was time to claim it. Tom was right; God's Word is the secure rope we have to tie us to the unmovable rock of Christ. Did you know that there are exactly 365 promises made to us by God? Amazing! What would our lives look like if we claimed one every day? I would expect that there would be a heck of a lot more secure people in this world, myself included.

As we looked back over the years and all the experiences that we had with our children, we found that God was there in each step; He has never dropped us. My husband and I recalled the time our son acquired such a deep infection in his toe that it required surgery. Then our oldest daughter required major knee surgery, and even our youngest had a traumatic procedure done to her foot when she was only five years old because she had gotten an extremely large and deeply embedded splinter from a wooden deck surrounding a pool while on vacation at her grandmother's. Of course those examples are not even the tip of the iceberg; I have not gotten into the falls, cuts, scrapes, burns, bumps, lumps, and bruises that go hand in hand with childhood. I hope that my point is coming across. Even when we felt we had no control in these trials, God was still fully in control. All these situations had good outcomes and we are so thankful for them. But even if these things had not gone well, the secure feeling we had was due to our faith that God had a plan and purpose for our lives and the lives of our children.

To bring our story back around and up-to-date is the issue Tom and I are currently facing. Together we are now letting our little ones, who are no longer little, go and allowing them to grow up. Some of their growing has been done in those formative first years, but the majority of the growth they will have is waiting just over the horizon. This type of growth can only be done through the living of life.

They will go to college—have moments of insecurity; start a career—have moments of insecurity; get married—have moments of insecurity; have children—have many moments of insecurity. Did you see a pattern? Our journey through life will consists of those times when we will be on high, clear mountaintops and other times when we will have to navigate through the darkest part of life's most uncertain valleys. It has been our goal to teach our children that their security should not be based on what's going on in their life but on how they react and to whom they are placing their trust when things around make them feel insecure. Tom and I have pointed our children in the direction of Jesus as the source of what can be relied upon in all moments. Our greatest challenge and privilege as parents have been raising our children to slowly let them go. Getting guidance from God's words and remembering everything He has done for us—every promise He has fulfilled in our lives—we have been attempting to realize this purpose: to entrust and pass down the same knowledge of the Lord to our children.

The biblical verse Deuteronomy 6:4-9 gives us confidence that we have done the best we could for our children. "Hear, Oh Israel! [Add your name to make it personal] The Lord is our God, the Lord alone. And you must love the Lord your God with all your heart, all your soul, and all your strength. And you must commit yourselves wholeheartedly to these commands I am giving you today. Repeat them again and again to your children. Talk about them when you are at home and when you are away on a journey, when you are lying down and when you are getting up again. Tie them to your hands as a reminder, and wear them on your forehead. Write them on the doorposts of your house and on your gates."

Tom and I have held fast to the belief that there is no greater security than that found in Christ and in a home where God is the Lord (Joshua 24:15b). God has hit this point home with us over and over again, but as I said earlier, never more so than in these recent months. To tie together all that we have shared: just the other week our girls brought home this year's school pictures. Tom was home early, which is a rare event, so he was able to enjoy looking at the pictures with everyone instead of finding a wallet-sized picture lying on his dresser. After they gave us the picture packets and we bonded over how great they turned out, the girls flitted off to grab a snack, do homework, or whatever else they do after school. The tradition in our home has been to place the current school picture over the one from the previous year. Tom and I were unaware of what a powerful moment we were about to encounter. We decided to take the frames down from the wall and change the pictures. It had been a while since we had looked at their pictures like this together. We marveled at our daughters' growth and made comments about some of the wonderful memories we each recalled. Then, we realized something as we skimmed over the pictures: this would be our daughter Jessica's second-to-last school picture. She only has one more year of high school left after this! Talk about a wave of fresh emotions crashing over you.

I instantly looked over at our son's picture. I missed his being home so much and realized that there would be no more school pictures for him. Kyle's childhood wall was complete. He is a college freshman, off on his own. But we took his pictures down anyway and went through each one as we had with the girls. When we were finished, Tom and I shared a sigh that needed no words. The meaning was clear, at least to us. There was a long look of love and security passing between us that expressed the feelings that have endured through 20 years of marriage and three children. That special look of love helps me stay secure in all we have done as parents and in our relationship. We have entrusted it all to God. He hasn't dropped us yet, and we do not expect the Lord ever will. This gives me tremendous security because as I end this chapter, Jessica's wall of pictures does not have much further to go and Montana, our youngest, is not far behind. No one knows what is ahead, but I can promise you there is no better assurance of security through the changes your life takes than knowing the One who does!

Questions For Your Spirit

- Explore your own sense of security: When do you feel most secure? When are you likely to be most insecure? What do you think makes you feel this way?

- Can you define what being secure means or looks like to you? Is it more important to be materially secure (having all the things you want) or spiritually secure (growing in a Christ-centered life)? What advice is given to us in Psalm 37:3-5 and in whom does it say we should trust?

- In moments of insecurity, to whom do you turn? What do you trust in to help you? Read Psalm 40:1-2. What security do we have if we build our lives on God's truth? Can the pressure of the world's demands ever crack the solid foundation of God's promises?

- Revelation 3:5 says: Those who endure in their faith have a secure place in heaven. Is that the security you want - an eternal place in heaven with Jesus? Does knowing that heaven is waiting for all who want it change your perspective about what you depend on to make your life secure? Before you answer, challenge yourself and read these scripture verses which reiterate the call of God to all people through

Jesus: Luke 11:1-2, Romans 10:13, John 5:24, and Matthew 14:23-33. Record any insights you may want to share or remember.

- When we need help in circumstances beyond our own abilities and control, what should we do? Spend some time meditating on Psalm 56:3-4, Psalm 60:12, and Psalm 61:2. Record how they build up the security that you can trust in and turn to God. When you face problems and temptations that are too big for you, will you let God show you the safe way out? Based on all that we read, can the security found in God ever be taken away?

Scripture to Celebrate

Amos 5:4, Leviticus 26:6, Ephesians 3:14-21, 1 Samuel 2:9, Psalm (23:4 & 139:3)

2 Corinthians 13:11, 2 Timothy 1:12, Matthew 6:33, Colossians 3:2, 1 Kings 8:56

What I Will Celebrate

What I Will Celebrate

Chapter Four:

Celebrate Being Significant in Christ

Celebrate God's Word – I knew you before I formed you in your mother's womb. Before you were born I set you apart and appointed you as my spokesman to the world. -Jeremiah 1:5

Think about this: God intentionally made you and me with great skill. With loving care, He crafted us. By the way He made us, God showed how much value He places on us. Every delicate inner part of our bodies was knit together in our mother's womb with God's full attention. Before we begin, consider how significant that makes you feel. I pray that you will continue to keep that idea at the front of your mind.

As Holy and as Righteous as God is, the message of the Bible is simpler than we think. I believe that He wants us to know that we are valued and significant. He loves us deeply. This is something that we will hear repeated many times because love is the center of God's character. God's love cannot be avoided; it is everywhere. His love is impossible to escape. We are given proof of this when we read Psalm 139. In verses 7-11, you will find this declaration: "Where can I go to escape from your Spirit? I can never get away from your presence! If I go up to heaven, you are there. If I go down to the place of the dead, you are there ... I could ask the darkness to hide me and the light around me to become night, but, even in the darkness, I cannot hide from you."

Do you now see a clearer picture of how significant you are to God? Keep in mind that we must not confuse our significance to God with the idea that we are sufficient without God. Our significance is found in God alone, and is tied to the value that He places on us. People matter to God. Thus, His continued presence in our lives demonstrates a strong and holy love for us. What we accomplish is not solely ours, but is by the gift of the work of Christ in us.

There are people who have never dared to dream of accomplishing more than what they thought they had the ability to do; they think that staying small and insignificant decreases the amount of disappointment they will have to face. From what I learned, it is not the failing that keeps us stopped; it is the lack of placing our hope in the direction which points to success. We sell ourselves short when we look at the small picture and our limited human view instead of the big picture of what can happen seeing it through the eyes of God. Hear this from the book of Jeremiah 29:11: "For I know the plans I have for you," says the Lord. "They are plans for good and not for disaster, to give you a future and a hope."

The celebration we experience comes only after we allow God's hand into our life. Once the Holy Spirit begins to work in us, we begin to accomplish great things and become significant for the purpose that God's plan holds for us. Being made significant in Christ will far exceed anything we could have envisioned. God carries us past our expectations and elevates us to His perspective. If you ever find yourself struggling with the need to be reassured that you really are significant to God, let Psalm 139:17 bring some of the encouragement you might need, "How precious are your thoughts about me, O God Almighty." There is no question that we are significant. Is it not incredible to know that our God thinks wonderful thoughts about you and me all the time? This verse has the ability to blow my mind, regardless of the number of times I come across it or think about it.

I don't know about you, but there is no way I am capable of thinking precious thoughts all the time about the people I know. It does not make me feel good saying it, but I will be honest. I find even doing that with those I love the most can be difficult sometimes. It is then I am called to remember that it is our humanness which makes God so awesome. Only by going to God and living in the love He gives, can we receive enough love to give to others. The meaning of significance in the spiritual sense is coming into agreement with God by understanding that we are significant not because of what we do or can do; we are significant because of what He gives and allows us to do.

Many of us become disheartened when we fight in our own strength to achieve what we have purposed our goals in life to be and only end up falling short of them. In those moments, it is important to realize that there is no such thing as being insignificant when we are living in close relationship to Christ, Jesus. This is a lie used to discourage us and leave us wondering if we are good enough. In fact; the lie of insignificance tells us we are not. God is thrilled when we come to the end of "ourselves" and reach for Him. This signifies a desire for a new start in becoming faithful to God. A sincere heart pleases God.

What we do with our time here on earth may seem insignificant and invisible. But, I promise you that if you use everything inside and outside of you to honor the Lord, it will be rewarded.

Ezekiel 18:20 backs up the promise that I just made: "...Righteous people will be rewarded for their own goodness." In addition to salvation, God promises also to reward those who love Him on the basis of their deeds. The principle for us is that God rejoices in what is right, not necessarily in what is big. Every life that has been created is significant. First, this is because our lives are gifts from God. One of my favorite quotes spoken by my mother-in-law is, "God does not make trash."

I have learned that we make our lives significant by choosing faith in the small opportunities presented to us. I challenge you to begin today, wherever you are right now, to do what you can. Accept God's pleasure over the smallest stride forward and you will head quickly in the right direction.

Insignificant to the world... Significant in the eyes of God - Looking at Mother Teresa:

Her personal sacrifices and contributions to the societies of the human race were noticed. In 1965, Pope Paul VI issued a decree which declared her group an International Religious Family. From a humble insignificant background, the Society of Missionaries has spread all over the world. They provide effective help to the poorest of the poor in a number of counties, and they offer relief when natural disasters occur or famine strikes. North America has also felt the significance of Mother Teresa's life. The Society of Missionaries has houses close to the United States where they take care of shut-ins, alcoholics, the homeless and AIDS sufferers. Because of a spark that was ignited in a young girl's heart, God used Mother Teresa's life in a significant way.

We have barely scratched the surface or in no way come close to touching upon all this life has done. This "blip" of a story is meant to go out and seek more of it. In other words, discover our own significance in what God has given to us. Recently my grandmother, at age 91, shared something very special with me while we were driving together in the car. We were talking about all the things God has helped her with throughout the years of her life and how faithful He has been. She said, "Giving my life to Jesus was the best thing I ever did. I have never regretted it for a minute. I talk to Him like a friend and He helps me." For someone to confess that she is where she is because of Jesus is so awesome. It shows me once again that God exists and He makes the life we have worth something…every time.

Mother Teresa's life went on to obtain many more recognitions and awards until her death on September 5,

1997. Her life is well marked throughout the world with great significance. The acolytes of man are not how she would want to be remembered. Her 87 years of life and 79 years of dedicated service to God and humanity were done because she allowed God to reach her heart and use her life as He designed. No one has benefited more so from her life than those she lovingly held in her arms on the filthy streets as they were dying.

"Life is an opportunity, benefit from it. Life is beauty, admire it. Life is bliss, taste it. Life is a dream, realize it. Life is a challenge, meet it. Life is a duty, complete it. Life is a game, play it."

"Life is a promise, fulfill it. Life is a struggle, accept it. Life is a tragedy, confront it. Life is an adventure, dare it. Life is luck, make it. Life is precious, do not destroy it. Life is life, fight for it."

(Mother Teresa)

References: 1. Facts about Mother Teresa – found on internet on Wikipedia, the free encyclopedia.

www.en.wikipedia.org

2. Quote by Mother Teresa – taken from Mother Teresa's Biography on the internet.

www.americancatholic.org

Questions For Your Spirit

- Are you aware of the significance of your life? Do you know what it is God gave you to do? If you do, thank Him…if you don't; pray and ask Him. Write any thoughts that God gives you to save or to share.

- Refer back to Mother Teresa's quote at the end of the chapter. What encouragement do you take from it? How does it make the insignificant little things in your life seem significant? Where do you think Mother Teresa looked to receive her significance? Are you able to say the same?

- Read 1Peter 2:5-10. How does this passage make us significant in Christ? What did God do through Jesus? What are the reasons for our celebration in Jesus?

- Like Mother Teresa's example, do you look for opportunities for God's mighty work or do you just see the obstacles as being so huge that they keep you stopped? A life of significance sometimes means we will have to take risks. Read Joshua 14:6-15. Record what you learn about Caleb when he finally realizes the purpose God gave him and learns to look past the size and strength of his enemies.

- The people around us can sometimes make us feel insignificant. It often leaves us discouraged if we don't know how to respond to this emotion. Have you ever had an experience where what someone said or did left you feeling insignificant and small? How did you handle that? Read Galatians 6:9 for encouragement and insight. This verse says we can avoid discouragement by keeping our eyes on the goal and reward of heaven. After all we have learned about being representative of Christ, would you view that experience differently if it had occurred today?

Scripture to Celebrate

James 3:13, 2 Corinthians 12:2-10, 1 Chronicles 28:20, Revelation 21:3-6, Ephesians 2:8-10

1 Corinthians 1:26-31, Psalm 40:2 & Psalm 1:1-3, Proverbs 23:4-5, Isaiah 5:1-7, John 15:13

What I Will Celebrate

What I Will Celebrate

Chapter Five:

Celebrate Being an Ambassador of Christ

Celebrate God's Word – Jesus came and told His disciples, "I have been given complete authority in heaven and on earth. Therefore, go and make disciples of all the nations, baptizing them in the name of the Father and the Son and the Holy Spirit. Teach these new disciples to obey all the commands I have given you. And be sure of this: I am with you always, even to the end of the age." – Matthew 28:18-20

The statement you have just read is known as The Great Commission; our "marching orders," if you will, from Jesus. His words convey the clear message that those who choose to follow His way have a definite job to do. Christians are called to action and instructed to enlist in God's army. Ours is not a passive faith. If we choose to accept it, our mission is to be Christ's ambassadors throughout the farthest corners of the world. Jesus gave us this charge as He prepared to leave this earth and we will spread His message until He returns again. This is the last time His friends would see Him face to face. Now it would be the Holy Spirit left with us to complete the work that Jesus left us to do.

At this point in history, Jesus had completed everything God had sent Him to do. He lived amongst us, taught us, loved us, befriended us, died for us, and rose from death to save us. Now, His Father was taking Him to the heights of Heaven to sit at His right hand (Matthew 26:64). The job now befalls upon His followers to remain faithful and complete the work He started. The Gospels (Matthew, Mark, Luke and John) are the eye witness accounts of Jesus' life. In the Gospels is where we meet the Son of God. It is in these writings that Jesus tells us who He is and what He was sent to do, and is where He personally invites us to become part of His family. Even before He entered the world, though, His coming was foretold and His mission destined.

One Sabbath, Jesus stood up and read from the Sacred Scriptures. This was a message that the Old Testament prophet, Isaiah, was given about the world's coming Savior: "The Spirit of the Lord is upon me, for He has appointed me to preach Good News to the poor. He has sent me to proclaim that the captives will be released, that the blind will see, that the downtrodden will be freed from their oppressors, and that the Lord's favor has come" (Luke 4:18-20). Once he had finished reading, Jesus rolled up the scroll and sat down. He then said, "This Scripture has come true today before your very eyes." That is what He was to do and what we now are about to be doing.

When Jesus called the original twelve disciples, His words were, "Come, be my disciple and I will show you how to fish for people" (Matthew 4:19). I believe that this means, "I will teach you how to tell people about me."

What Jesus is asking is for us to be His ambassadors. Look up the definition of ambassador. You probably will encounter several terms related to the word 'GO'. To be an ambassador literally means: 'one who goes on an errand'. This person is an interpreter, messenger and representative of which they were sent. The concept of being an ambassador is not a new one. All through the pages of the Bible we witness people being called for a holy purpose or in keeping with the definition, 'those who were sent on an errand'. Some of the more familiar examples from the Old Testament are the people God sent. God asked Noah if he would build an ark for Him. (Genesis 6) God asked Moses if he would lead the people for Him. (Exodus 3&4) God asked Isaiah if he would go to the people and speak for Him. (Isaiah 6) There are several more stories like that. Some of God's requests are bold such as the ones we just shared and some requests are subtle and spoken only in the soft places of our hearts. Either way, the Spirit commands us. God lets us know when He wants us to listen. The point I'm stating is each of these men were sent by God in a different direction but with one common goal. Leading people to friendship with the Lord and joyfully announcing His presence to the world.

Another interesting fact that I picked up on is an ambassador does not "go" with his or her own agenda. Their only motive is ensuring that every effort is put forth to successfully accomplish the job they were chosen to complete. Jesus clarifies that point when He said, "The truth is, anyone who believes in me will do the same works I have done, and even greater works, because I am going to be with my Father." (John 14:12) We must remember to follow the ultimate role model. Jesus asks no more of His followers than to imitate the things He did. Through Christ, God has given us the privilege and authority to tell people everywhere what God has done for them. (Romans 1:5) You are among those who have been called to belong to Jesus Christ, dear friends. God loves you dearly, and He has called you to be His very own people. (Romans 1:6) Is that not a reason to celebrate? God has called you to be an ambassador of Christ!

Here is where I believe many of us get confused. We think that as an ambassador of Christ, we need to head for the deepest part of some unknown jungle in some far away third world land with the hope of changing the world (or at least that part of it). Actually, doing just that is part of being an ambassador of Christ. We cannot argue that there are a lot of people in desperate need that is beyond our limited comprehension in this lost and hurting world. Extreme poverty, cruel suppression, war, sickness, natural disasters, and violent conditions continually plague our globe as a daily reality for so many people. The impact of the enormous contributions that the thousands of missionaries and organizations have made across the nations in the name of Christ to ease this suffering is evident. Even when the cost has meant their lives and other selfless sacrifices, those who serve as missionaries in other countries have heard and responded to Jesus' command to go. Jesus placed importance on traveling in order to reach the people. Much of His time was spent healing the sick, teaching the seeking, and saving the souls of those in the cities He visited. But, the other option is that we can stay right where we are and still fulfill the mission of making disciples. Jesus desires to be in our everyday conversations. It should be as natural as sharing a cup of coffee with our friends.

In the book of Matthew (23:11), Jesus says, "The greatest among you must be a servant." Being an ambassador is like being the personal servant of God. It really doesn't matter where our mission field is as long as we approach our mission with the attitude of Christ. Being a good witness to Jesus is what the role of ambassador is all about, no matter where they are stationed. It is letting the light of His love shine bright in your life so that it can be spread into the life of another (John 8:12). Once that light catches into enough hearts, you have a movement and revival powerful enough to transform the darkest areas of any place you are at. All around us, in our schools, workplaces, churches, communities, neighborhoods, and families, there are opportunities for us to be used in influencing lives for the Kingdom of Heaven. Jesus goes on to caution us that though the needs of humanity are many, those stepping up to make a difference are few. There is desperate need for workers. Our works matter to God, for our work as Christian ambassadors brings Him glory.

Jesus traveled through cities and villages teaching and announcing the Good News about the Kingdom. Wherever He went He healed people of every sort of disease and illness. He felt great pity for the crowds that came because they had so many problems and they did not know where to go for help. They were like sheep without a shepherd. He said to His disciples, "The harvest is so great, but the workers are so few. So pray to the Lord who is in charge of the harvest; ask Him to send out more workers for His fields." (Paraphrased from Matthew 9:36-38) Wow, what a challenge Jesus left us with! Are we ready and willing to meet it? Would these be the words you would want Jesus to say to you? "Who did you help?" "Who did you tell about me so that they may be invited into eternity?" "I wanted to send you, but you did not go." Or would you like to hear Jesus say to you, "Well done, my good and faithful servant. You have been faithful in handling this task, so now I will give you many more responsibilities. Let's celebrate together" (Matthew 25:21). Jesus makes no demands; He only invites us to be His disciples.

Jessica's story:

From what I have understood through the reading of Scripture, the only criteria necessary to be an ambassador for Christ is having a heart aligned with His. Nowhere in the Bible did I read about any stipulations based upon race, gender, social class, or age in order to be used for Kingdom work. God has room for anyone willing to answer His calls—even a teenager. Several names quickly ran through my mind of young people being used as God's ambassadors. Maybe you are familiar with them, too. King David was only a young teen when God used him to win the battle with a giant and defeat the Philistines. (1 Samuel 17:32-48). Then there was Josiah who at age 8 was Jerusalem's king for 31 years (2 Kings 22:1-7). Perhaps the teen that was to be used in the greatest capacity to bring God's message to the world was the mother of Jesus. Mary was a young girl when the angel of the Lord appeared to her and announced the job God wanted to give her. She accepted with humility the role she was to fulfill (Luke 1:26-38). These are just a few examples to emphasis that God can use who He wants, when He wants to deliver the message He wants. Our job as ambassadors of the Lord is to be obedient to the call we are given.

We might never be asked to fight a giant or rule a nation but I can promise you that God can use each one of us to make His presence known in this world. Nothing is too small to escape God's attention. Our daughter Jessica is someone who has taken the role of Christ's ambassador to heart. She joyfully celebrates what she does. Jessica is a teenager who is passionate about sharing the love of Jesus with little children and puts much effort and care into introducing them to who He is. Her work with the youngest of God's future disciples is the mission field she has been lead to for right now. Even when Jessica is not in a "church" setting, we have observed her making it a priority to be a good influence for those little ones who are watching and learning from her. It does not matter if it is being asked to babysit or teach a Sunday school class; Jessica serves where she is needed.

She understands what Jesus said, "…Anyone who welcomes a little child like this on my behalf is welcoming me…" (Matthew 18:5-6). Jesus' words teach us that God is pleased when we nurture the faith of a child.

Jessica started helping out in the Sunday school program when she was 13. Over the past four years God has used her to touch the lives of not only the children, but the adults that she has worked with as well. They have all noticed her unmistakable gift for teaching and sharing God's word. Jessica's personal relationship with and love for the Lord is what inspires her to be a part of something she feels is important. Not many 17-year-old people place a high emphasis on getting up early every Sunday morning and spending two hours with toddlers and pre-school age children. Dedication is also part of being an ambassador and Jessica has definitely mastered that principle. I love watching her diligently prepare her lessons and get special treats ready, bought with money she has made by babysitting, to give the children. Her motive is purely to pass on what she knows about Jesus. God has blessed her commitment. Jessica is no longer just a helper, but God has made it possible for her to have her own class and also teach at Vacation Bible School in the summer.

It is in the everyday things of life that God wants to use us, because that is what most of our lives consist of, the everyday living. If a child's life has been changed by receiving the love of Jesus in a Sunday school class, then that class has been well taught. Being an ambassador means being available to go where we are needed and have the best opportunities to connect with people. I look forward to watching all that God has planned to do through Jessica, in her journey with Him. He has only just begun to use her young life as an instrument through which people have already become exposed to Jesus. Every Christian is an ambassador of Christ to a non-believing world. God gives us the privilege and responsibility to speak and witness to others. Our actions are, in themselves, a testimony to the world.

Questions For Your Spirit

- Refer to the words of Jesus in Romans 1:8 – "But when the Holy Spirit has come upon you, you will receive power and will tell people about me everywhere." What do you learn in this verse about being an ambassador of Christ? What enables us to become effective witnesses for Jesus?

- Read 2 Corinthians 5:18-21. Are you allowing God to use you as His ambassador? If so, how are you being used? What have some of your experiences of telling others about Jesus been like?

- Re-read Matthew 28:18-20. Take a few minutes, and think about the challenge we are given. In your own words, re-state what Jesus is asking. Are you fulfilling The Great Commission in your life? Who are you discipling (teaching)? If you are not currently journeying with someone in his or her faith, would you consider asking God to put someone in your life to disciple? Do you feel you need someone to disciple you? Are you bold enough to ask so that you can receive this?

- The Bible clearly teaches us, as Christ's ambassadors and as Christians, that we must be ready to tell the stories of how we met Jesus and how we experience His presence in our lives. We must share with others the message of the Good News we have and the truth about Jesus. This is both our privilege and responsibility (reference Romans 1:14-17 and Ephesians 4:17-25). What is the story you have been given to tell?

- Colossians 3:16-17 says, "Let the words of Christ, in all their richness, live in your hearts and make you wise. Use His words to teach and counsel each other...And whatever you do or say, let it be a representative of the Lord Jesus, all the while giving thanks through Him to God the Father."

What a powerful verse! As ambassadors of Christ, we are to use His words and knowledge to teach others. What personal challenges were revealed to you as you read the words of this verse? Are you prepared to represent the Lord with whatever you do or say? Spend some time in prayer before you answer. Let God search your heart for the answer, then write down what is revealed. Use Psalm 139:1-6 and 23-24 to help guide you in prayer. As you seek to know God better in your life, ask Him to point out what He wants you to understand.

Scripture to Celebrate

1 John 2:12-15, Revelation 4:9-11, Romans 12:10, Daniel 12:3, Isaiah 6:8-10, Jonah 3

Ruth 1:14-16, John 18:28-38, Matthew 9:10-12, Malachi 4:2, 1 Corinthians 14:1-4

What I Will Celebrate

What I Will Celebrate

Chapter Six:

Celebrate Resting In Christ

Celebrate God's Word – "On the seventh day, having finished His task, God rested from all His work. And God blessed the seventh day and declared it holy, because it was the day when He rested from His work of creation." - Genesis 2:1-3

Before taking a look at what it means to rest and the principles we should take and apply into our own lives from our understanding of it, let's consider the opening verse right from the conception of creation. It really amazes me that God begins His relationships with everything He has brought into being with rest. Why would the omnipotent (all-powerful) God of the entire universe rest after completing the work of his creation? The answer is not because the Almighty ran out of steam. He was not physically tired, nor was His intention to simply end work. Our clue lies in the words we read. God, in ceasing from His work for a period of time, called His rest "holy."

He knew, before we did, our necessity to cease from our work to nurture our spiritual and physical needs. Work is good, but our mortal bodies, unlike God's, get tired. God leads by example and allows rest to be part of His character. We, too, must regularly balance our attention between our health and the well-being of our souls. I pray that what we are about to discover in God's word together will inspire us to observe regular times for worship and spiritual refreshment.

If someone were to tell you that rest is important, what would your first reaction be? Would you seriously consider the topic, or would you quickly dismiss it because you are too busy to be detained by what seems to be such a meaningless conversation? It is likely that the majority of us would respond, "Who can afford to take the time to rest with so much to do?" Honestly, that is true for me. I lead a fast-paced, purpose-driven, and goal-oriented life. My goal is to complete my daily "to-do" list by checking off each task. To rest before everything is done is very difficult for me because stopping is not an option I am open to. Being transparent with our difficulties is not always comfortable. I am able to admit that because we all have growth areas in our lives. The concept of being free to celebrate "rest" is, without a doubt, an area I need to improve. I plan to do so with the help of God's Holy Spirit. As humans we are limited in our ability to battle our weaknesses. It is hoped for us that as we become aware of our weaknesses, God's strength is emphasized (2 Corinthians 12:2-10).

Do not be too hard on yourself if this idea of taking time to rest is bigger than you can currently handle. It is necessary for us to put everything into perspective before we can manage to change, if, of course, that is what we want to do for ourselves. It is easy to become confused about what mind-sets we should formulate. On one hand, we feel vaguely guilty if we relax, but on the other we, for some reason, feel a sense of pride when we explain to each other how busy we are. No wonder such internal turmoil mixes around in us. We live in an age of high stress and anxiety levels, and this is most likely due to the momentum of rocket-like speed at which everything in our society moves. Does it surprise you how challenging it can be to think about the importance of rest in a different way? It almost feels impossible for those whom are always on the go and who feel the need to be in constant motion. How can we celebrate something that we have a hard time experiencing, or do not fully comprehend?

To assist us in understanding this concept, we should know that the type of resting that God speaks about has nothing to do with being lazy or unproductive. The rest He speaks of restores our souls, refreshes our spirit, rejuvenates our bodies, and restores our relationship with Him. In Psalm 23:1-3, we read about how we can begin to have that experience of refreshment which God promises…He lets me rest in green meadows, He leads me beside peaceful streams, and He renews my strength. It is clear from these words that God did not intend for His people to live in a state of perpetual hurry and worry. For this to become relevant in our lives, we must continually refer back to God's example in Genesis that flows into the message of the New Testament. Through His Son Jesus, God wants us to discover rest and refreshment for our body and soul. As we choose to respond to this and follow Jesus even more closely, we will then encounter both the richness of His rest and refreshment because of His presence.

Jesus said to us in the book of Matthew 11:28-30, words which may be familiar… "Come to Me, all of you who are weary and carry heavy burdens, and I will give you rest." This is something that truly should give us cause to celebrate if we grasp what is being offered here. What Jesus wants to do is relieve our burdens and lead us into a life of peace and rest. Does that sound like what you are looking for? Is the thought of rest becoming more appealing now that we hear God wants us to have it? The final and ultimate rest is found in the eternal promise waiting in heaven for those who put their faith in Jesus. For all who enter into God's rest will find rest from all their labors. (Reference: Hebrews 4:1-11) Far more than rest from work; God longs for each of us to be filled with the rest supplied by His peace.

The peace He gives is the gift that Jesus left which surpasses all human understanding. (John 14:27) This peace guards our hearts and our minds as we live fully alive and rest in Christ Jesus. (Philippians 4:7) What we now should decide is, if God saw rest as holy, how can we afford not to rest?

Jesus…takes time to rest? (Mark 1:29-38)

The balance between rest and productivity is something I think will continue to remain a struggle within our American culture as well as within many other cultures. We have already talked about the speed we move at and the pace things are accomplished. People can accept the importance of spending time regenerating; but doing it? This is what is difficult to concede. The mind-set of "business" distracts us from finding the inner peace of rest that a Spiritual relationship with God will bring us. Our fear is those important tasks awaiting our attention may not get done if we don't keep going.

We have already established that resting is more than just stopping what you are doing. God wants us to turn away from the voices of the "world" and tune into His Spirit so we can spend that time to hear Him. We are not only physically made but God created us with spiritual needs as well. Believe it. Our souls actually thrive with rest. (Proverbs 4:21-23) The question which plagues us once again is…how can I do this with all the responsibilities I have to accomplish? My experience is that this is the "spirit" our age seems to relate to and functions in. Action! Fast moving action! Take a quick test for yourself. How often do you find yourself having these thoughts? How fast can I get there? How soon can I get the job done? How can I keep things moving? Which statements are true for you? Does it surprise you that the topic of rest does not appear to come up often? The good news for us is that even if we do not fully understand how to incorporate this concept into our personal lives and make it practical, we have the model of Jesus and His behavior to guide us. We can celebrate the fact that each time we turn to God's word, there is something meaningful waiting there to benefit us and possibly change our situation, if we allow it to. The pages of the Bible are where God first begins to teach us and to open our hearts so He can speak to us. It is also the place where we find Jesus and see the things He did and understand what it is He can do.

Mary Barrett

The life of Jesus is the road map leading to God for those who desire to follow that path as closely as they are able. The Gospel of Mark is a book written in a style that everyone can relate to. We might even want to refer to this book as the "Gospel of Action," because it is filled with stories both of miracles and actions. These stories prove beyond a doubt that though Jesus came in order to be a servant to the world, He was not merely a man. Only God's Son could do the things recorded here. For the most part, the focus is on Jesus' actions, rather than His teachings. It flows like a video, a moving picture that draws us in, as we become involved with the life of Jesus. Mark is my favorite Gospel because it speaks to today's practical world and is perfect for the hectic lives we lead. We find the servant Jesus, as Mark portrays Him, deeply interested in our workaday world. Jesus is the working person's Lord and Savior because He was actively in contact with people. Jesus spent His days involved in what people were doing and cared about the things they cared about. He was not some unknown or unapproachable theologian separated and seated in cross judgment of us. (John 3:16-17) Jesus was always found working with those around Him.

In the portion of Mark we are referring to, Jesus has been up and actively doing things. Chapter one, verses 29-38 shows us a very busy day. Jesus has been healing the sick of all kinds of diseases and ministering to the well-being of those being victimized by evil spirits. The next day He was to preach in Galilee. With this tight schedule, you might expect Jesus to hit the floor running; racing to get to the next thing on His list. But, in verse 38, lies the lesson for us...The next morning Jesus awoke long

84

before day break and went out alone into the wilderness to pray. Interesting, with all that was still yet to be done, Jesus took the time to retreat and rest in communion with God? Several things are revealed in this short sentence. First, resting does not always mean that we are asleep; it also includes the intentional act of setting the time apart to get into a secluded place to be uninterrupted. Second, rest ultimately is about refocusing on the things ahead so that you are prepared and equipped to handle them. Third, the only way that our Spirit can truly be at rest is for us to spend time with the One who created it. God knows us best and wants our connection with Him to be strong and alive; not dull and weak. Praying is our active life-line to our Heavenly Father. For that to be productive, we must nurture it with quiet fellowship and quality time alone. Jesus knew this better than anyone. Although there are many ways to rest, Jesus understood that the most important aspect of rest is keeping us close to God.

What else can be said? Life is life, but how we approach it is always our choice. The philosophy of Jesus was to be a servant who faithfully does the will of his master. The will of God is to obey Him and serve others; which Jesus did perfectly. This should be our goal as we journey through life. Rest is a command of God for our good. He knows the pressures we are under and the way we tend to exceed our physical limits. As we contemplate all we have read and strive to apply some of what we have learned, let us keep these words of Jesus with us as a challenge to inspire us when we need to take time to stop. Then Jesus said, "Let us get away from the crowds for a while and rest." (Mark 6:30-31)

Questions For Your Spirit

- Read Exodus 20:8-11. How important is God's command of rest to you? Do you set apart a time and make it holy between you and God? Are you careful to observe the celebration of worshiping the Lord with the gift of your time and attention?

- Is finding refreshment for your mind, body and soul a priority or is rest something you wish you had time to do? What type of rest do you think Jesus was talking about when we refer back to the passage of scripture in Matthew 11:28-30? Have you gone to Jesus yet to find the rest you need?

- What effect or benefits do you think would be experienced if we lived in the habit of regularly resting? Do you think that this type of change is even possible in your life?

- Make a list of the things that keep you busy. Is time alone with God on that list? Can this list be altered? If it could, how drastically would it be revised? Pray over the lists you made, and ask God to expose to you the things which are keeping you distracted and tied up. Challenge yourself to make a new list that has been influenced by the counsel of God's spirit.

- <u>For personal growth and deeper thought</u>—the true celebration of resting in Jesus comes from developing a lifelong relationship with Him. Jesus is where our soul finds acceptance, love, peace, counsel, healing, restoring, and rest from the daily demands of life. We are free to just "be" as we are when we are walking close to God. My prayer has been to just place a new thought on your perspective of how important spending time resting is to every aspect of our existence. But, I wanted to give it to you from God's definition. The time we have on earth is short. But, it can be so precious if we live it with a Christ centered mind and a heart open to the love of God. Reflect on these words of scripture and write down what they mean to you. May they speak truth and bring rest to your spirit as you piece them together to make life worth living.

Psalm 39:4-6: "Lord, remind me how brief my time on earth will be. Remind me that my days are numbered, and that my life is fleeting away. My life is no longer than the width of my hand. An entire lifetime is just a moment to you; human existence is but a breath. We are merely moving shadows, and all our busyness ends in nothing. We store up wealth for someone else to spend."

Scripture to Celebrate

John 5:39-40, Psalm 77:4-6, Mark 3:1-6, Ephesians 4:20-24, Isaiah 57:15, Ecclesiastes 2:17-26

Psalm 103, Nehemiah 8:11-12, Hosea 14:4-9, 1 Timothy 4:4-5, Leviticus 23:25, Jude 1:1-2

What I Will Celebrate

What I Will Celebrate

Chapter Seven:

Celebrate Following Christ

Celebrate God's Word – Then He said to coward, "If any of you wants to be my follower, you must put aside your selfish ambition, shoulder your cross daily, and follow me." - Luke 9:23

Following Jesus is a call to holy living and the hope of eternal life. To determine whether or not you will place Jesus at the center of your life involves a choice. In order to follow Him, a definite decision to go in a certain direction must be made. That direction entails leaving our old habits and bad behaviors and trading them for the patterns and path of Jesus. To make a good choice, we need to first fully comprehend what following Jesus means. Our attempt will be to answer the specific question; what would it take and what would it look like for us to become committed followers of Christ?

To follow someone or something usually begins with the desire to imitate what you see. We emulate the examples of certain lifestyle principles or people that have made an impression on us by doing what it is they do or valuing what it is they contribute in some way. But, following Jesus is more than just a fleeting phase or what's considered the most popular fade at the moment. In order to follow Christ, we need something with a little more depth than just wanting to do it. Your journey walking with Jesus begins only with a willing heart. Take that well into consideration before taking your first step and agreeing to follow. A willing heart comes at a personal expense. This means we must think less about what we are leaving behind and more about what we must pick up so that we can follow effectively. Everything else stays behind if we choose to move forward and make the commitment to devote ourselves whole-heartedly to following Jesus. He explained this to us Himself in Luke 9:24: "If you try to keep your life for yourself, you will lose it. But if you give up your life for me, you will find true life."

The New Testament books of the Bible teach us first and foremost that God wants us to follow Jesus before anything else in our lives. To anyone familiar with Scripture at all, this makes sense. Consider the structure of this logic. Christians believe that Jesus Christ is the perfect Son of God. Christians also believe that God sent Jesus to save the world He loved and the people He created so that we could have a place in eternity by following Him. Doesn't it seem right to go in His direction? Only then will we end up at His destination – heaven. The goal of Christians is to follow the path which leads us to eternal life and union with God forever. Read John14:1-7 for yourself, and be certain that you know where that path begins and ends. Is this the road that you are already on?

God will never force us to follow, but He is always waiting with the invitation to join Him.

The cost of following Jesus will be difficult at times. Our convictions and beliefs will be put to the test because we are asked to no longer live a life that is controlled by the nature of the flesh, but, to concentrate on being influenced by the righteousness of the Spirit. 2 Corinthians 5:17 says, "Those who become Christians become new persons. They are not the same anymore, for the old life is gone. And new life has begun!" The reason anyone decides to follow Jesus is because they want to be reconciled to God and have believed His message about the coming of the Kingdom of God. Once, our relationship with God was damaged beyond repair. We were powerless to undo the separation which sin placed between us and God. In His grace, God did not leave us there. He reached us through Jesus. Christ's shed blood blotted out our sins and reconciled our friendship with God. This is salvation; we are no longer under spiritual death, judgment, and darkness but we are raised in a new life to follow Jesus; saved to have a second chance at what no longer is a broken relationship with our heavenly Father. For those of us who have received this gift, it is the most natural thing to want to celebrate and share the good news of following Jesus with people who need to know the relief of what it means to be reconciled with God. We need to think carefully about all that Jesus has said about our intentions to follow Him. We know already that our eyes are to be on Him for the glory of God and off our own ambitions. In Luke 9:25 Jesus says, "And how do you benefit if you gain the whole world but lose or forfeit your soul in the process?"

Jesus is making the point that if a person is unwilling to follow Him faithfully and is ashamed of sharing His message, He will also be ashamed to recognize that person when He returns to earth in all His glory to claim everything that is His (Luke 9:26). Do not be fooled to believe that it is possible to somewhat follow Jesus. He gives several clear warnings about this. There are three of them that come quickly to my mind. As you read each illustration, look for the caution contained in each one.

1. Luke 9:59-60 — He said to another person, "Come, be my disciple." The man agreed, but he said, "Lord, first let me return home and bury my father." Jesus replied, "Let those who are spiritually dead care for their own dead. Your duty is to go and preach the coming of the Kingdom of God."

2. Luke 9:61-62 — Another said, "Yes, Lord, I will follow you, but first let me say goodbye to my family." But Jesus told him, "Anyone who puts a hand to the plow (or begins to follow Jesus — emphasis mine) and then looks back is not fit for the Kingdom of God."

3. Luke 16:13 — No one can serve two masters. For you will hate one and love the other, or be devoted to one and despise the other. You cannot serve both God and money.

The common thread running through the whole idea of following Jesus is wrapped around the word loyalty. Loyalty, by definition, is the unwavering commitment without deviation. This is the crucial element asked by Jesus from people who are saying they want to follow Him. If you claim loyalty to God, you cannot attach yourself to anything that takes your priority over God. You are either totally sold out to following Jesus or you are not. Divided loyalty is not accepted. God expresses His loyalty to us by refusing to give up on us no matter how we disappoint Him with our sins. We can express our loyalty back to God through obedience to His words and following His Son's example in this world. Our proclamation should be the same as this: I will go wherever you go and live wherever you live. Your people will be my people, and your God will be my God (Ruth 1:14-16). So, what have you decided? Are you better equipped now to become a follower of Jesus and celebrate the journey to where He leads? What is the direction you have chosen? Will you be the captain of your own ship or will you turn the voyage over to the One who already has plotted and traveled the course? Following is not done just by walking in blind obedience when being asked to. Jesus has already proven Himself to the world and has revealed His light so that man can see! May you open your eyes and be blessed as you decide wisely what important things are those which you choose to follow. I pray that these words will be claimed and true for you: choose today whom you will serve (follow)…But as for me and my family, we will serve (follow) the Lord (Joshua 24:15).

Whom have you noticed?

We learn about Jesus, of course, when we read the Bible and go to church to hear sermons. As a person growing in a Christian way of life, I have learned that the best way to really know who He is in our daily lives is by observing the lives of others who claim to follow Him. We can have the opportunity to see who Jesus is through the people who have been placed in our circle of family, community and friends. It is hard to just pick one person to hone in on. Jesus says that He lives in everyone who chooses to follow Him. One example stating this is found in John 15:1-17 where Jesus tells us that He is the true vine we need to connect with in order for our lives to be productive. Therefore, we all have the responsibility to represent Him to the world and reflect Him in our living.

I know for me I have the blessing of being in the company of many who follow Jesus and have a relationship walking closely with Him in faith. To watch how they follow Jesus as a daily practice has been a source of encouragement, inspiration and motivation for me. Even more awesome is that four of them live in my own home. Watching my children grow and mature as young Christians and the deeper level of prayer and worship my husband has come to understand has added much too how I see the power of Jesus and God's goodness working. Using that as a challenge, I try to do my best to represent positive spiritual qualities to them. The vision of the Mother in Love Series became a reality because I noticed something different in someone's life and was drawn to finding out about it. When we follow Jesus just by living it as He did, people do notice. By our quiet actions of service, unconditional loving heart, dedicated deeds, commitment to the standards of God and a habit of worship to the King of heaven, we influence the lives of others to want to transform to what Jesus offers. Those were exactly the things which I saw in the life of my mother-in-law.

At first, it was not what she said that struck my interest, but her behavior toward her Lord and Savior. Her love for Jesus radiated inside her and spilled out around her. It is difficult for us as humans to portray every characteristic of Jesus. Jesus was made fully human as we are, but He is also fully God, which means that He is perfect. His perfection in us is the only resource we have available to please God or to be worthy enough to follow Him. It is for that reason that to write about one person whom I thought followed Jesus flawlessly seemed impossible for me. The examples of good I have witnessed in so many people have taught me that God magnifies our strengths so that we can grow and touch others in various ways. Our personal strengths, abilities and talents are called Spiritual gifts. God has given us each different ones in order to accomplish great things for Him and to help us enjoy life. Deep within the human spirit are the desire and capability to do wonderful things. Our goal is to first identify our abilities, then to exercise them, and finally to channel them toward good rather than evil. This has been what I have told my children often over the years as they have been growing up.

My idea is to share how what I have noticed in others has helped to build my confidence and commitment to want to follow Jesus in my life. I would like to introduce you to a few special people whose walk with Jesus has affected mine. The relationship with my mother-in-law has been the one that has profoundly shaped my Christian life. The time we had together is something I will always be thankful for, and will treasure as a priceless gift. At age 23, I started following Jesus as my Savior because of her introducing me to Him through what He had done in her life. I decided I wanted that, too. She prayed with me so that I could ask Jesus to come into my heart and forgive my past sins; I began a new life with a changed spirit within me. Details of all that was shared with me are described throughout the five books contained in this devotional series. That is part of my journey; the intention of following Jesus is to also be growing and changing with the experiences you encounter along the way. Over the years, other lives that God has brought into contact with mine have been meaningful to me as I matured in my faith.

If you have been following the Mother in Love Series, you have probably already noticed the tremendous inspiration that my husband and three children have given to me as I have watched them over the years. A lot of the stories I have shared are ones that tell how I saw them following Jesus. But, the value of contributions from my five sisters-in-law, sister, family friends and father-in-law cannot be ignored. I have noticed a different spiritual gift in each of them. Much of where I am today spiritually is the result of staying close to people who have the same bedrock beliefs about faith. I have learned not to be closed-minded, but rather to be ready to do the work in the world that God asks us to do. For several reasons the gals I "hang" with the most are my sisters-in-laws. We are connected by serving in the ministry of reaching other women for Christ. Most of us also attend a weekly Community Bible study and often spend time in home fellowship. Therefore I will tell you about them first.

We are all at different stages and places, both in our personal and spiritual lives, but when you are focused on the Lord these things do not matter; we all bring something to the table. Betty Ann is the one who shows me that part of following Jesus involves needing His mercy as He is the only One who can lead you to the mercy seat of God's throne. That mercy is what she counts on each day to get her through. Rita is the one we call the group's "Berean." Her slow, wise decisions have been an example to me, showing me that we must know God's Word and use discernment before we act. As Jesus knew and trusted the Father, so must we. There is no arguing with her about God's Word; if He says it, she believes it! Janet opens her heart and home to anyone who needs a friend. The lost and lonely are welcomed at her door. The words, "love your neighbor" are evident in all she has done for people by giving a loving place of shelter when it was asked of her. She sets the standard of hospitality that I aspire to reach. In my sister-in-law, Terry, there has been a dedicated commitment to her run her household and raise her children in all diligence to the standards given to us in the Bible. Finally, there is Margie. She is my partner in speaking at the conferences we run for women to attend. She possesses the ability to teach God's Word in a way that the ladies relate to and help them get what Jesus is saying. Through these women, I have witnessed many faces of Jesus and see the beauty of a life that following Him grows.

I also alluded to a few other people as inspirational examples. My sister Beth is just a few years into her spiritual journey as a Christian. It has been remarkable to see the change that following Jesus has begun in not only her life, but in her marriage and with her children. Ever since she gave her life to the Lord, she has been actively pursuing more of His ways. Her home is filled with new peace because she has found joy that was not there in the same way as it is now. There are so many ways open to us to show Jesus in our lives to others and to live by the principles He taught. We all do it in our own way and in our own time.

So far each person has brought out a different trait of Jesus. This is also true of my father-in-law; he follows Jesus by being the shepherd of his family. Before He was taken to heaven, we know that Jesus spent some time with His closest followers. He included them in where He was going, eventually. But He left them work to do while they waited to be called home. In His final earthly moments, Jesus talked with Peter and their conversation went like this: Jesus said, "…do you love me?" Grieving, Peter answered, "Lord, you know I love you." Jesus said, "Then feed my sheep." He then went on to tell Peter some more about the ways he would be used to glorify God. Jesus ended the conversation by saying, "Follow me" (John 21:17-19). My father-in-law is one who feeds his sheep. Dad has ten grown children, and some of them have struggled terribly. But whatever Dad's own situation, he has never once turned any of us away when we have asked for his help. And his selflessness in taking care of others extends far beyond his own family. Countless others have been helped in times of crucial need because my father-in-law responds to Jesus' call to take care of others, both physically and financially.

From my reading of the Gospels, I believe that Jesus wanted what was important to Him to be important to us. Through these little descriptions of some modern-day saints, we have seen how much these people do and follow the things that Jesus considers important. Prayer is high on that list. Jesus' habit of staying in constant communication with His heavenly Father was never broken. Prayer cannot be separated from the nature of Jesus; it is to be consistent and persistent. In Matthew 6:5-13, we find Jesus giving His disciples the pattern they are to follow when they pray. The topic of prayer continues and is repeated throughout all the Scriptures because that is the way we get to talk to God. Between my mother-in-law and her best friend, Mrs. Kempf, I have seen what following Jesus in a life of prayer looks like. These two ladies shared a partnership of daily prayer together that spanned over thirty years. Not only have I seen what it looks like, but my family and I have been the recipients, numerous times, of the incredible blessings of prayer. Even though Mom is no longer with us, Mrs. Kempf, is still the person we go to when we need a prayer warrior. She continues the battle of faithful prayer by asking God for guidance and waiting for His leading and direction; she does not move without it. There is so much covering the legacy that was laid on the foundation of prayer between Mrs. Kempf and my mother-in-law. All the details of the lives affected by their diligence cannot be covered by a brief summary like this. What I learned from them is that prayer is an act of humble worship in which we seek God with all our hearts. Because of that, I now follow a life of prayer with Jesus. II Chronicles 7:14 is a special verse to me and sums up the kind of prayer that God is pleased with. "Then if my people who are called by my name will humble themselves and pray and seek my face and turn from their wicked ways, I will hear from heaven…"

That is what I can share from the experiences I had about the way I have come to understand how to follow Jesus. It has brought me to the place I am at today. I promise you that every time you look for Jesus with all your heart, you will find Him, even in the lives of others. Keep these key ideas in mind to guide you before you decide what gets your attention. Where have you been looking? Whom have you been noticing? Does it lead you to following Jesus?

Questions For Your Spirit

- Do you know what you following after? Revisit the verse in Joshua 24:15 - ...choose today whom you will serve... But as for me and my family, we will serve the Lord. How would you finish this sentence? But as for me, I will serve_____.

- The story in this chapter shared specific examples of how some people are following Jesus in their lives. What characteristics that show that people are following Him have you seen in the lives of people you know? What are some examples that you believe you have shown them?

- Following Jesus means leaving everything else behind and devoting our lives to Him. How are you devoting yourself to following Jesus? What things are you intentionally leaving behind to follow Him? Leaving things behind does not have to mean leaving people. It also means changing habits and behavior in our lives that keep us from effectively following Jesus.

- Psalm 119:10-11 says, I have tried my best to find you – don't let me wander from your commands. I have hidden your word in my heart that I might not sin against you. How do you think this verse relates to the things we need to know about how to follow Jesus?

- Psalm 119:59-60 expresses a very personal, wholehearted commitment to follow Jesus. If following Jesus is your desire, are you willing to make these words your prayer? "I pondered the direction of my life, and I turned to follow your statutes. I will hurry, without lingering, to obey your commands."

Meditate on them carefully before you do. What do they stir in your heart? Write down what inspires or encourages you.

Scripture to Celebrate

Exodus 23:24, Galatians 4:9, 1 Corinthians 1:19-21, John 16:5-11, Romans 3:9-16, Galatians 6:7-8

Judges 17:6, Deuteronomy 10:12-13, Matthew 6:33, Psalm 55:22, Mark 14:38, Isaiah 57:12-13

What I Will Celebrate

What I Will Celebrate

Chapter Eight:

Celebrate Overcoming In Christ

Celebrate God's Word – "I have told you all this so that you may have peace in me. Here on earth you will have many trials and sorrows. But take heart, because I have overcome the world." John 16:33

Jesus says, "I have overcome the world." Wow, what a statement of complete victory! What if I were to tell you that we have the capability to also overcome the world? Would you believe me? Does it seem impossible to look past what's defeating you at the moment? If you are interested in trading your trials and sorrows for the peace of Christ, start by laying them at His feet. The first step to overcoming the world is taking a step towards Jesus. Nothing brings me more hope than knowing we can overcome every situation we are in through Christ's victory over death. He did indeed overcome the world through His resurrection. It is because of this that we too can conquer any difficult situation. Just with that brief introduction, does it excite you to know that we can celebrate and experience spiritual victory over sin, death, or whatever else that attempts to set itself up against us? In Christ, we already have a victory far greater and more lasting than the things we can earn in this temporary world. The expectation of reaching heaven exceeds the grandeur of anything man can put together. Christ's victory of overcoming the adversity and hatred of the world and its darkness is the triumph we are promised by remaining close to His side. The Bible paints a picture of the final, glorious victory that all who overcomes this world will receive. Engrave these words of our Savior into your heart and begin to become more and more encouraged that you have victory awaiting: "All who overcome will be clothed in white. I will never erase their names from the Book of Life, but I will announce before My Father and His angels that they are mine.""Anyone who is willing should listen to the Spirit and understand what it is saying to the churches" (Revelation 3:5-6).

This is a fairly straightforward subject for us. We either choose to overcome our obstacles, or we are overcome by them. We can only be defeated if we let it happen. Sometimes we will fail in what we try to do. The difference is that failure encourages us to try again, while defeat keeps us stuck where we are. To overcome has been well explained as "courage stretched out." Do you ever wonder why it seems that no matter what we do, we cannot get past a certain circumstance? We learn by reading God's word that although He does deliver His people from difficult and painful times, He often waits until they realize that they depend on His presence in their lives. It is during this test period that our faith is strengthened and our courage is built up. Enduring faithfulness is how we begin the process of overcoming every fiery trial that life throws at us. Our main purpose is not to suffer in silence, or to be beat up, but to come out on the other side of our problems with obedience, hope, and joy. Understanding how to overcome our problems and celebrate our victories in Christ, no matter how big or small, hinges on our willingness to be steadfast in living lives of faith. As the Bible points out, in fact, faith devoid of the commitment to continue to the end, despite the hardship or battle you are engaged in, is considered dead (James 2:14-17). The Book of James 1:2-4 helps clarify this for us: "Dear brothers and sisters, whenever trouble comes your way, let it be an opportunity for joy."

For when your faith is tested, your endurance has a chance to grow. So let it grow, for when your endurance is fully developed, you will be strong in character and ready for anything.

How great does it feel when you complete a challenging project, excel in a difficult task, or are relieved of a stressful problem? If you have not yet known such a feeling, don't be discouraged. I can tell you it can be obtained. I refer to this passage in the Book of Philippians 4: 11-13 almost daily to keep me focus on the truth about what I need in order to be victorious. Read this with me "I have learned to get along happily whether I have much or little…I have learned the secret of living in every situation…For I can do everything through with the help of Christ who gives me the strength I need." For those who have learned the same secret, you will find that it provides not just strength to overcome. Centering Jesus as the source of your life will empower you to be successful and overcome any situation.

The Apostle Paul likens the idea of overcoming the trials we face to the philosophy of finishing a race. Think about everything that it takes to not just win a race, but too complete it. It takes dedication, discipline, and desire. To win a race, we must not stop. To have victory, we must never give up. The key word we have been using is "endurance." Just to get to the end with the intention to overcome the physical, emotional, and mental fatigue requires finishing strong. There is not much difference in running the spiritual race that is ahead of all of us. Paul says we must keep pressing towards the goal of living to fill God's plan for our life. He writes, "I don't mean to say that I have already achieved these things or that I have already achieved perfection! But I keep working toward that day when I finally will be all that Christ Jesus saved me for and wants me to be... I am still not all I should be, but I am focusing all my energies on this one thing... I strain to reach the end of the race and receive the prize for which God, through Christ, is calling us up to heaven... We are citizens of heaven, where the Lord Jesus lives... He will take these weak mortal bodies of ours and change them into glorious bodies like His own... using the same mighty power that He will use to conquer everything, everywhere" (Philippians 3:12-21).

Ask yourself this, "Do I have the faith it takes to make it to the end?" "Will I trust in Jesus so that I can overcome my challenges and complete the race in His power?" "Do I want the rewards God promises for those who overcome?" If your answers are yes or you want them to be, than let us

celebrate these words together, "We are looking forwa
to the new heavens and new earth He has promised,
world where everyone is right with God" (2 Peter 3:13)

"I now pronounce you husband and wife…" Now what?

Sharing our "love" story:

We will tell the stories we know well the best. What we ar
familiar with is of course what we are comfortable with
We do not have to live through someone's exact situatior
in order to receive something from their message or find
something to relate to. When things touch our heart and
shape who we are; that is our story. Our stories have a
purpose. Every life is a story and every story, a lesson. By
simply utilizing our personal strengths, we can benefit
others and hopefully give someone a bigger picture into
something they are struggling with. The stories I know
best are my own. Through these stories of inspirational
writings, I have weaved through some of the chapters
snapshots of my life. I have used my battle with anorexia,
my husband, and each of our three children to help show
the practical side of living a Christian life. I have shared
our failures, struggles, and successes as proof that we are
nowhere near perfect. My prayer has been to express that
it has been God's perfection and presence in our lives that
has sustained us and has never once failed.

Overcoming something is not just focused on the
end result of victory, although that is part of it. Rather, it
is looking back over the journey it took to get there and
feeling appreciation for where you are. I believe that if we
just want to win a challenge to "beat" something, we will
quickly forget the battle, but, if we want to win so that

we can achieve being closer to God and gaining more and more of the things He has for us, then the battle takes on a whole new meaning. The victory we obtain from that is even sweeter because we have moved towards the goal of heavenly rewards, which last forever. I shared all that because I cherish my marriage above anything else I have in this world, but, if I am being honest, Tom and I had to overcome a lot of hard things to get to the place we are after twenty years. It is now as we look back over what God has allowed us to overcome that we have a deeper gratitude for Him and each other. We believe without a doubt that even though it has not always been pretty we were given a special kind of love; one that says, "...till death do us part."

This part of my story will be letting you into the lives of two nineteen year old kids who were set on getting married. These two thought they knew what they were doing and exactly how it was they were going to do it. Not yet to the altar, one could bet on at least a few obstacles that are standing in the way -just looking for trouble. It all started at age fifteen and a half when Tom asked me to be his girlfriend. He was extremely cute and treated me nice, so what's a girl to do? I became his girlfriend. We dated for three years and almost right after graduation, Tom asked me to become his wife. We wasted, or to be accurate -I wasted no time in planning our wedding. We were engaged for exactly one year and two months, not that I was keeping track. The big day arrived on April 21, 1990. Everything was perfect! What could go wrong? This was too easy. We were well on our way to "happily ever after." Uh-huh. Then the alarm clock went off and we woke up a few months later to a much different side

of the story. Reality, the part they don't tell you about…
or was it that part that our parents told us about, but we
were going to do it anyway? Either way, we were faced
with… now what?

Tom and I are about as different as two people can
be. In fact, Tom is tall, measuring at a height of about
six feet, whereas I am height-impaired. On a good day,
with my hair done just high enough, I measure up to an
impressive four feet, 11 ½ inches. At times we thought
that it was just a cruel joke to be so different. I have a
few more examples. When he is hot, I am cold. I love the
beach, and Tom would be perfectly happy never stepping
foot on sand again. Of course, that is precisely how I feel
about the great outdoors, with all of its bugs and dirt! Our
personalities and the ways we do things clash noticeably
at times. We know first-hand what miscommunication,
misunderstanding, and misinterpretation are all about.
When we are not on the same page, it feels like we are
not even reading the same book! These problems are
not uncommon in marriage or any relationships. They
certainly can set themselves up as major issues to be
overcome. We all want the "better" out of the deal, but
what do you do with the "worse"? For those two lovesick
young people, it took quite a few years to figure out.

Let's face it; our individual quirks can tend to be
irritating and downright annoying. For some people, they
can even be cause enough to terminate a relationship.
That was never an option for Tom and me. He mentioned
several times during our engagement that if I didn't want
to go through with marrying him, I could end it at any
point before walking down the aisle. Once the "I do's"

were said, it was done forever. That in itself was a huge commitment. Tom's view of marriage was already set in his mind by the example he saw in his parents' marriage, and I believe he was unsure at first about what my view was. Even in this area, our backgrounds differed. My parents were divorced when I was eight. My two sisters and I were raised by three loving parents, because my mother re-married. To us, traveling between two homes was normal.

Think about how the institution of marriage has changed over the years. Generations ago it was unthinkable to divorce, no matter what the situation was. You were expected to find a way to overcome it. In our current day and age, you simply try marriage on. There seems to be this catching attitude of, "no worries, if I don't like it, then I don't have to stay." It is unthinkable in today's society that we should be unhappy. We like the idea of playing house for a while, but only until it stops being fun or we lose interest. In God's eyes it is not possible to get away with a cavalier attitude about the importance of relationships, especially the ones He blesses through the union of marriage. In the book of Matthew 19:4-6 it says, "...since they are no longer two but one, let no one separate them, for God has joined them together."

The point is not to analyze the reasons why marriages do and don't work, or to find a way to control the alarming rate of divorce, because it is not possible. Tom and I have found only one way to overcome the painful and devastating times in our marriage and come through them together, and that is to put our trust in Jesus to get us through. We both have given our hearts to the Lord, and that connection with Him has bonded our marriage together in a very precious way. The long list of things that separate us is nothing compared to our shared source of hope.

It is living by godly values that have had the greatest impact in our marriage and parenting style. Jesus said that our actions give away our value system. What we do shows what we really believe. (Luke 6:45) Our love story is definitely tied into the love we have been shown by God.

This unpredictable road we are on is one in which I know we are sharing with everyone else. Who has not had financial hardships, serious health concerns, or fair share of emotional heartache? Sometimes it is almost enough to cause you to give up, is it not? Each story carries with it its own pain and none is less valid then another. Although we may not face the same exact burden, we all need to overcome the obstacles that are put in our way and their attempts to hurt us. For us, it has been overcoming issues with addictions, health, employment, finances, and personality conflicts and to be totally transparent, the desire to continue to fight. Tom and I are stronger today then we were those twenty long years ago because we have learned to turn to the Lord and not take on our problems alone. God's people are those who recognize His powerful works of deliverance. Because of the healing God has brought into our lives, on many occasions we have experienced these words, "Come and see what our God has done, what awesome miracles He does for His people!" (Psalm 66: 5-7) He has moved major mountains for us by keeping a roof over our heads, food on the table, healing my sickness and literally restoring eye sight. We have overcome much by the undeserved favor of the Lord. Each time I was tempted to take my eyes away, I remember the things our God can do.

I look forward to what has not yet been written in our love story. I believe I speak for both Tom and myself when I say that we will continue to strive to live by these words to ensure that our marriage will be a wonderful testimony of overcoming the adversities of the world by holding onto God's standards: "Give honor to marriage, and remain faithful to one another" (Hebrews 13:4). If you still struggle with how to overcome victoriously your strongholds, let this final passage of Scripture be your encouragement and your challenge as you consider restructuring your life: "Continue to build your lives on the foundation of your holy faith and continue to pray as you are directed by the Holy Spirit" (Jude 1:20). May God bless you as the Holy Spirit strengthens your faith through prayer.

Questions For Your Spirit

- 1 John 5:4 – "For every child of God defeats this evil world by trusting Christ to give them victory." What three words in this passage tell us how to overcome evil? How does this encourage you? Do you believe that through Jesus you can overcome and defeat your personal battles so that you ultimately can claim victory in your life?

- Have you experienced God's victory in your life? What in your life do you still have to overcome? Make a list of what your struggles are and, if you are ready, offer them as a sincere prayer to the Lord. Read Romans 7:24-25 to assure you that our answers are found in Jesus Christ, our Lord.

- Ephesians 6:10-18 explains the armor of God's protection. This passage's clear message is that we are to wear that armor every day to protect us from the evil we cannot see. What is each piece of armor we are to wear? What is the purpose of each piece? How does this help us overcome whatever comes up against us?

- Has there been someone in your life who has inspired you by their example of courage in the face of great odds? What do you think was their source of strength to help them overcome their battle?

- Hebrews 2:18: "Since He (Jesus) Himself has gone through suffering and temptation, He is able to help us when we are being tempted." This verse helps us remember that Jesus suffered for us on the cross. How might knowing that help us when we want to quit the race? To be an over-comer we must keep our eyes fixed on the compassionate love and care from God to see us to the end. What are some things you could do or are doing that keep you focused on Jesus so that you can come strongly across that finish line?

Scripture To Celebrate

Exodus 33:14, Romans 8:17-18, Psalm 126:5-6 & 103:2-9, Jeremiah 6:27-30, 2 Corinthians 12:7-9

Ezekiel 22:1-16, Colossians 3:2, Job 19:25, Genesis 39:3, 1 Peter 5:10, Luke 11:28, Hebrews 4:16

What I Will Celebrate

What I Will Celebrate

Chapter Nine:

Celebrate Your Inheritance Through Christ

Celebrate God's Word - For if we are faithful to the end, trusting God just as firmly as when we first believed, we will share in all that belongs to Christ. – Hebrews 3:14

The inheritance we will be defining is a spiritual inheritance. It has nothing to do with waiting till someone is dead to receive what is coming to us, nor does it have anything to do with a reading of a will, per say. There are no lawyers involved, no fees to be paid (Jesus took care of that); no fighting with siblings over what is rightfully theirs. Our inheritance is written in God's Word. He is clear and exact about who is worthy of this inheritance and how it must be obtained. There is certain criteria for being included in the inheritance God wants to give us, but, it is not saved for a select few. Anyone who wants to be a part of God's family is invited to become heirs in all His glorious heavenly riches. (Revelations 11:18)

A Spiritual inheritance is that which is embodied in the celebration believers have as heirs of God and joint heirs with Christ. Because God has adopted each one of us into His family through salvation in Christ, we share joint and equal heir-ship with His only Son. Unbelievable, we get what Jesus has been promised by His Father. Jesus is already a participator in the family possessions and if we are in union with Him, so are we. In this inheritance, the Father does not die but lives on forever in His family. Although He is physically absent, He is ever spiritually present in His children. The phrase "the heirs of God" presents a most vivid picture of the eternal and intimate relationship between the believer and God. This union is the faithful soul's possession in this present reality. For those experiencing this part of the inheritance, they do not merely have to wait in anticipation of the Kingdom of God on earth or in heaven; it is to be lived today. For the child of God, there is much to be received by our heavenly Father. This inheritance cannot be disputed, over turned or taken away by any court in the land because it is without price and cannot be passed on to anyone who is not in the family of God. (Matthew 25:1-13)

Evidence of who are considered members of God's household and are entitled to His inheritance is found in Hebrews 3:1-6: "And so, dear brothers and sisters who belong to God and are bound for heaven, think about this Jesus whom we declare to be God's Messenger and High Priest. For He was faithful to God, who appointed Him, just as Moses served faithfully and was entrusted with God's entire house … For every house has a builder, but God is the one who made everything … But Christ, the faithful Son, was in charge of the entire household. And we are God's household, if we keep up our courage and remain confident in our hope in Christ!"

One of the greatest gifts we are offered as an inheritance from our heavenly Father is a promised place to rest. This place of rest is equal to, and also considered as being in, His presence and fellowship. God's promise for us to receive this place of rest will stand until He sends Jesus back for all of His children still on Earth. The Good News is that God has prepared a place of rest, and this has been announced to everyone. Sadly, although this place was created when God made the world, those who do not believe what they hear will not choose this inheritance. God has set the time for us to enter this place of rest as today. For only we who join God's family will be written in His "will" (referenced throughout Hebrews 4:6). If you want to claim this inheritance, today you must listen to God's voice. Do not harden your hearts against Him (Hebrews 4:7).

Most of us are already familiar with what an inheritance is; someone we love has left us something special for our benefit. I remember the Christmas my Grandmother left a very generous portion of money to her seven grandchildren, their spouses, and her 19 great-grandchildren as our inheritance. She was 90 at the time and wanted to see the joy that this would bring to each of us. Mom-mom wanted to share the moment with us, so she made sure she was still with us to do it. Knowing that she was able to be a blessing to us also gave her happiness. I believe this is the same way with God. He desires to give good gifts to His children (refer to Matthew 7:9-11) because He wants to celebrate everything that a life transformed by receiving His inheritance will bring, which is eternity spent with Him. No matter how often we have heard John 3:16 repeated or have read it again and again ourselves, it still remains the only reason why we can celebrate our inheritance from Christ. Let the words sink into your heart like new. Perhaps you may be claiming this scripture for the first time as a sincere prayer of wanting to accept the inheritance Jesus came to give you: For God so loved the world that He gave His only Son, so that everyone who believes in Him will not perish but have eternal life!

I have noticed that so many things we have expire and become unusable. There are expiration dates on food, promotional sales and coupons. God and the love He offers is not that way. We don't ever have to worry that God's inheritance will expire or that we will miss out. Although it does benefit us to include Jesus in our lives right now, He is waiting to be asked. Those benefits are the experience of the fruit of the Holy Spirit, namely love, joy, peace, patience, kindness, goodness, faithfulness, gentleness and self-control. We can thereby live according to a new life and celebration in Christ. (Galatians 5:22-23) The gift of this inheritance is as fresh and alive as it has always been and will be; you, dear people, are the children of that promise. Christ has set us free, so we must make sure that we stay free. We live in the freedom of our inheritance, accepted by God because of our faith. Make sure that you stay free and do not get tied up any longer by things of the past. Only those who are free can share in this! (Paraphrased from Galatians 4:28-31)

Our inheritance - Foretold + Announced + Delivered = Jesus:

As we look at the story of how our inheritance of fully being God's children was offered to the world and how it entered, be careful to keep in mind all that an inheritance is. Remember that an inheritance is not a reward, nor something that can be earned by working for it. An inheritance is something received based solely upon who you are. A birthright is your place in a family because you were born into it. Anything the family accumulates is shared with those who are of the same bloodline. If salvation and the blood of Jesus has put us in His royal bloodline, then we would be wise to learn as much as we can about our heritage and what exactly being part of this family tree is all about. Christians believe that all life began in the Garden of Eden and extended from there. That was the old covenant understanding of bloodline, where the consequence of sin called for payment.

To explain simply, we are part of the new covenant where God promised Abraham that through His descendants would come the One who was to be the payment for all man's sin. (Genesis 15) Throughout the Old Testament, there are stories of prophets preparing the way and foretelling the people that our inheritance to the Kingdom of Heaven was indeed on His way. As we examine the three areas in which our Spiritual family tree was planted and grown, it is important to take note that God has taken the time to make sure that everyone is included. He writes our names as His beloved children.

Foretold

The prophet Isaiah paints a wonderful picture of the coming of the Messiah and His everlasting Kingdom of justice, righteousness, and salvation, which are the inheritances God's people long for. These are the future joys and blessings that will one day come to those who remain faithful to the Lord. There are interesting parallels between the Old Testament's Book of Isaiah and the New Testament. Jesus is presented in the last 27 chapters of the God's revelation to Isaiah, as well as in the 27 books of the New Testament, which are about the life of Christ and His followers.

Anyone who has ever traced their family tree to uncover their roots understands that you need to go back as far as you can. Since we are in the "foretold" stage of exploring our family tree in Christ, we will go back to Isaiah 53:1-12. Walk with me through these verses as we continue to discover that a life of faith in Christ entitles us to the everlasting treasures of Heaven. The story starts when the Lord says that He will one day send His Suffering Servant to the world. His life was made to be used as an offering for sin. It is because of His sacrifice that He will have a multitude of children, many heirs. The Lord's plan will prosper in His hands. God has said that He is satisfied with all that would be accomplished by the anguish of His Servant. He will make many righteous. The saving power of the Lord will be revealed to those who believe in this message.

Thus, we know that God planned for those who were separated from Him to be made part of His family through the suffering of His perfect Servant.

Announced

My motive with this search to "find" the origin of our spiritual inheritance through these three different areas has been to inspire more people to want this. Those of us who already actively participate in this experience can live in full celebration because we know that we have a Father whom we can always believe in. Whether our parents are the greatest or the worst on earth, God is our Heavenly Father who never disappoints, who is always right, who is always fair, who always loves us, and who never leaves. Even those on earth whom we love and who love us are not perfect. Our human DNA is all the same and has limits. God fills in everything that we lack. He has a special place in His heart for those who are lonely or abandoned. Psalm 68:3-6 says, "God is a Father to the fatherless."

God announced in a very unique way that He was sending a Son. He did not send a messenger or a stranger. He needed to gather His family and He knew His Son would take care of family business.

It was to be through the Son that God would save His family and entitle them to partake in the inheritance which would carry His name. If we accept this inheritance, we too are given the name Child of the Most High God. The birth announcement is made. A long time ago in the small city of Nazareth, the Angel of the Lord appears to a young girl and speaks. Mary is asked to bring forth the Inheritance of Man into the world. God wants her to be the mother of His Son.

We know that this announcement contained the way in which we would inherit eternity. Mary tried to remove the confusion that raced in her mind about what the angel could be saying to her. Gabriel (the angel of the Lord) explained … "God has found favor with you and has decided to bless you! You will become pregnant and have a son, and you are to name Him Jesus. He will be very great and be called Son of the Most High."(Luke 1:26-32) She is then told everything that the Son would get. God will give Him the throne of His ancestor David. And He will rule forever and His Kingdom will never end. (Luke 1:32-33) From reading 2 Samuel 1:1-2:7, we find out that David becomes king over Judah. So, the inheritance of royalty is also promised.

This is the story of the human dimensions of Jesus. He is called the Son of Man because He was the ideal person for the job of bringing us to God. Nothing about Him, not even His conception was defiled. Our inheritance is pure. Listen to the rest of the announcement. Mary was still worried about how this all was to happen. She asked the angel, "How can I have a baby? I am a virgin?" There was no delay in the reply, "The Holy Spirit will come upon you, and the power of the Most High will overshadow you. So the baby born to you will be holy and called The Son of God…For nothing is impossible for God." (Luke 1:35-37)

That is a lot to handle, especially for a young girl. That job was saved for Mary. None of us will ever have that opportunity; but, like Mary, we all must decide if we believe the announcement that God brought His Son into the world for us, to save us and to give us everything waiting for Him by the Father.

Peace also is now there for us, my friends. We know that our inheritance has been foretold to us - announced to us. Are you ready to have what is promised delivered?

Delivered

You would think that an inheritance which carries such a dynamic magnitude and great wealth with it would first be made known to the greatest in the land when it arrived. That is not at all how our God works. He extends His best gifts and most generous mercies to those who love Him most and know Him best. The lowly soul, who has an open heart, will always be the one who see and receives the treasures of heaven. On the night God delivered the blessed inheritance of His Son into the world, it was not the Kings, the wealthy or the noblest of the land which saw the great light; nor did they hear the heavens rejoice. It was only a cold field filled some shepherds and flock of sheep which were chosen to witness such a miracle. The radiance of the Lord's glory suddenly appeared around them.

Again, an angel of the Lord spoke to reassure the frightened men of all they were seeing: "Don't be afraid! I bring you good news of great joy for everyone! The Savior-yes, the Messiah, the Lord – has been born tonight..." (Luke 2:8-11). The promised bloodline of the Lord was now extended into the world. The shepherds ran to the village as directed by the angel and found the baby lying in the manger used by animals. Our greatest inheritance was discovered in the most humble of surroundings.

While they were there, the shepherds told everyone what had happened and what the angel had said to them about this child (Luke 2:16-17).

Mary heard everything that the shepherds said about her sweet, little, newborn baby boy. Everyone else who heard the same things were astonished also, but she quietly treasured these things in her heart and thought about them often. What is really interesting is that Mary was not the only one who had this gift announced to her. Her husband, Joseph, and an old man named Simeon were also among the privileged few. Joseph had the announcement of Jesus brought to him in the middle of the night. God spoke to him in a dream and told him to marry Mary. Joseph reacted in quiet acceptance of all that was placed upon him. This was not the case when the two young parents brought Jesus to the Temple to be circumcised, according to the Jewish custom for all boys eight days after their birth.

The Holy Spirit had revealed to a man named Simeon that he would not die until he saw God's promised Savior delivered. He was a righteous and devout man of God who waited expectantly to lay eyes on the inheritance of the world. What a life of celebration he must have lived because he believed what God said as the truth! Simeon was there when Mary and Joseph entered the Temple in Jerusalem to present the baby. He recognized them right away and wasted not a moment. Simeon took the child in his arms and praised God saying, "Lord, now I can die in peace! As you have promised me, I have seen the Savior you have given to all people. He is a light to reveal God to the nations, and He is the glory of your people Israel!"

As Simeon blessed them, he said to Mary, "This child will be rejected by many in Israel, and it will be their undoing. But, He will be the greatest joy to many others…" (Luke 2:21-35)

The third piece has been given to us in the form of a helpless baby and two people who were just getting the idea of what God has blessed them with. This family would have the eyes of the world on them as the ones God chose to deliver the Good News of His kingdom. These are not the only three pieces of evidence that reflect our inheritance being found in Christ. God's Word is saturated with wonderful stories and lessons from cover to cover as to why we should long to celebrate the inheritance that comes from Him. These examples were the clearest and the most familiar to many of us. They were used to find a starting point and follow it all the way home to eternity where we receive once and for all everything the Father wants to give us. But, remember to begin by living in what you already have been given today. Be very excited that God wants to give you all He has simply because He loves you as His child.

There you have it, a spiritual inheritance which has been foretold, announced and delivered by God and those points to His Son, Jesus.

Questions For Your Spirit

- Have you ever thought of accepting the salvation of Christ as an inheritance? What is your definition of an inheritance?

- It is possible for us to lose our earthly inheritances. People can write us out of their will and consider us no longer part of their family. How is God's inheritance different? Can we ever lose a spiritual inheritance or be kicked out of God's family because of something we have done? Refer to Psalm 103:11-12 to reflect on your answer. Record any other scripture you know or have found that share the same thoughts.

- If the idea behind a spiritual inheritance is to be offered a new life in Christ where we can celebrate freedom from sin, how does Romans 6:1-11 say we are actually able to become free from the power of sin? Write down what you learn. Look for a clue in these words as part of the answer to what we need to do to defeat sin: So you should consider yourselves dead to sin and able to live for the glory of God.

- 1 Thessalonians 5:10 says, "He died for us so that we can live with Him forever, whether we are dead or alive at the time of His return." How does this verse encourage us that we are saved for a future hope by an inheritance that does not expire? Part of what God wants to give us is hope for the future. What a wonderful gift to know that we do not have to worry about where we are going after our time on earth is done. What a comfort it is to know that God is already here for us while we are living on earth. We have an inheritance that we can use both before and after we die. While here on earth we learn that we can walk in the newness of life and that for those who are saved, the death of the body holds no power.

- For personal thought: If we have such a marvelous inheritance through Christ's bloodline and God's promise that He will satisfy all of our needs, why do so many people (more and more every day) seem so unhappy? Meditate on the following Scriptures as you ponder this question: Matthew 5:3 – "God blesses those who realize their need for Him, for the Kingdom of Heaven is given to them" and Ecclesiastes 1:8-11 – "No matter how much we see, we are never satisfied. No matter how much we hear, we are not content…"

Scripture to Celebrate

Colossians 3:1-4, Malachi 3:6-7, John 5:39-40 & John 11:25, Proverbs 3:10-13, Psalm 8, Acts 2:38

2 Thessalonians 3:4-5, Genesis 15:4-8, Deuteronomy 2:7, Amos 5:4, Mark 10:29-31,Luke 2:41-51

What I Will Celebrate

What I Will Celebrate

Chapter Ten:

Celebrate Establishing a Godly Heritage

Celebrate God's Word – There you and your families will feast in the presence of the Lord, your God, and you will rejoice in all you have accomplished because He has blessed you – Deuteronomy 12:7.

One of the greatest privileges of family life is to assure the continuity of the family and its ideals, especially God's presence within the family throughout its generations. Faith in God is the most important part of a heritage that we can pass along to our family members and to future generations. Psalm 102:28 promises that if we raise our children in the faith of following Jesus, the result will be that their children's children will also thrive in the presence of the Lord.

From the beginning, the structure of a strong family unit was God's intention. Our families are where we first learn about the essential principles of life. If a family is rooted in a deep spiritual heritage, there can be no greater institution with a more positive effect on the world. There is no better place for the truths of God's Word to be taught and modeled. Ephesians 6:1-4 explains to us that we have the responsibility to bring our families up with the discipline and instruction approved by the Lord. Establishing a Godly heritage for our family means to love them, discipline them when necessary, teach them proper conduct, and be good role models for them. By sharing our own spiritual experiences, as well as the Word of God, they will be reminded of their spiritual heritage. If we fail to lead our families towards spiritual truths, their relationship with God is impacted and the heritage of faith is jeopardized.

The Bible talks about an earthly family as being made up of husband, wife and usually children for the purpose of being united together by the band of faith in Christ. In some books of the Bible there are lists of several genealogies recorded by family units. This was done to show the family as central and fundamental to the development of people and nations. The common factor in each genealogy that accomplished great things for the Lord had its foundation built upon a Godly heritage. The family is one of God's greatest resources for communicating His truth and inspiring change in any community of people. This change is directly related to the family's spiritual upbringing, commitment, and zeal for the Lord. The Godly heritage of any family starts with its spiritual training and having the gospel of Jesus explained to them.

Do you understand how important the family is and how every aspect of society is affected by the type of heritage that we pass down? Does it make sense to claim that our identities, origins, cultural orientations, and beliefs all stem from the family unit? The role that each individual plays in the family is vital, quite literally, to its survival and prosperity. Each member's behavior and contributions can have either positive or negative impacts on the family. The consequences of behavior usually determine if a family will function as a healthy unit or become dysfunctional. The book of Proverbs provides an example of a positive role model working for the good of the family to ensure that a heritage of Godly values is instilled. Proverbs 31:10-30 describes the attributes of a wife of noble character and is well worth the time it takes to read it in its entirety. However, I would like to highlight a list of words used to describe the type of character that this person possesses: virtuous, capable, precious, trustworthy, busy, energetic, strong, hard worker, servant, compassionate, fearless, dignified, wise, kind, and God-fearing. I hope that you have seen some of these traits in yourself.

On the other hand, we also need to know what happens when a family does not follow in the ways of the Lord. We are warned about the negative consequences for a family that fails to care for each member and to pass on a healthy, spiritual heritage: "But those who won't care for their own relatives, especially those living in the same household, have denied what we believe" (1 Timothy 5:8).

Such people are worse than non-believers. This is a strong caution, because we know that only believers can be part of God's family; those who claim to be His must be careful how they interact with the family God gave us here on earth. As God abundantly cares for us, so should we joyfully care for and serve our own families. I will not make a list of the negative words we associate with callous behavior. I am sure we already know what hurtful behavior looks like. Some of us can relate to the heartache that is caused by families living in turmoil and out of touch with God.

The goal of a Godly heritage is to extend the qualities of God's family to our family and all of the lives we come in contact with. The statement that we make by our words, actions and deeds will flow into the lives of our family. What are you saying with your life? What type of heritage are you leaving for the generations that will follow? What is to be remembered because you were here? The only way we can bring God's love to the world is to live it and celebrate what He has done and will do for us each day! I can promise that living a life that celebrates this will extend to the lives of others. You can prepare today to make sure that this happens by following the instructions that the Apostle Peter gives us. I have used this verse many times before, but it fits perfectly here. These are the most important things we can do for our families, and the best way we can treat them: "Finally, all of you should be of one mind, full of sympathy toward one another, loving one another with tender hearts and humble minds." (1 Peter 3:8) And because you have acted this way, you will be blessed with this result if you remain faithful and stay close to Christ . . . You will be able to tell wonderful stories to your children and grandchildren about the marvelous things God is doing . . . (Exodus 10:2). Praise the Lord for the gift of His Heritage, which we have to pass along; may we be challenged to do it well!

Betty's Spiritual Legacy in my words:

In many respects, the Godly Heritage I have received started when I was young. I had parents who took me to church, and I certainly grew up knowing who God was. We come from generations of Catholic background. Both of my grandmothers set examples for me of praying and sharing the customs of their faith. They had their roots deeply planted in religion, and they followed the rules. One of my grandmothers actually lived in Italy until she was 21, and my maternal grandmother was the first generation of Irish immigrants in her family to be born in America. So, as you can see, tradition cannot be separated from the cultures they lived in. I learned the Catholic traditions, and what was considered proper reverence to God, well as a child. Everything that was taught to me as part of my Godly Heritage put me on a good path for a while.

When I became a teenager, my views on religion quickly changed. Church was no longer a requirement my parents adhered to. It was up to us to choose whether to go, and for a long time, I chose not to. Most of this may sound familiar—it is the typical way it goes for the majority of us as we navigate our way through life. I didn't know many people with deep-seated Christian roots that actually determined how they lived. That was of course until I started dating the young boy who would one day become my husband. I would learn very early in our relationship that his mother did not just live her faith when it suited her, but she lived it as often as she could.

Her standard was set by the Lord and it could not be lowered. As I began getting to know her over the years I was dating her son, she was always friendly, warm, and had an incredible smile and hug waiting every time I saw her, but I knew something was different about her. The very first thing I ever noticed about the woman who became my mother-in-law was that her home was run very differently to the way mine was. My husband and I had similarities in our childhood upbringing, but on the topic of spiritual heritage, it was totally different. His mother did not give religion to her ten children; she modeled an intimate relationship with Jesus Christ as Lord and Savior. Betty taught all those close to her by the way she lived her life that through Jesus you had a clear path to God with no man in the middle. Establishing that part of a Godly heritage happened before I even met my husband. This has blessed our home by providing a man ready to be the head of the house because he fears and knows the Lord. Tom loves me and the children and is a dedicated husband and father because of what his parents taught him. These are now the exact values that we have raised our children with and pray will continue to be passed to their children.

I was so blessed to have been able to spend eighteen years with her before God called her home. She was who I watched as my mother in the Lord. Her commitment to God's Word and her unwavering loyalty to serving Him affected me greatly. When I was a newlywed and new to being a mother, the things I noticed about her life were the things I began to desire in my own. So, I began to talk to her about it. I was realizing that I needed God in a much different way than I did before. I was drawn to the relationship she had with Jesus and the way she so openly shared what her faith was all about. The Godly heritage that she extended to me has been the gift of showing me how to love God, my husband, my children and my home as first priorities.

The best testimony we have is how we use our lives. If people look at us and see the image of Christ reflected, that is the highest honor we can bring to God. My mother-in-law lived the Scripture. The legacy of being a Christian woman is what she left me. The verse she has forever connected me to is being a Titus 2 example to the generations to come which says: "But as for you, promote the kind of living that reflects right teaching". (Titus 2:1) This is what the Mother in Love Series is founded on and its message is echoed throughout each book. Titus is a book in the Bible with very strong focus on a person's character. It contains practical advice about what makes a Christian an effective leader. These leadership qualities will indeed promote right teachings which lead to right living if instilled into our life and lived out for others to be influenced by. Being a good example for others in your family and community to look up to is the easiest way to explain leadership qualities. She not only was totally committed to doing what was right, but encouraged people to want to do what was right.

My mother-in-law left different legacies for everyone who knew and loved her. Her Godly heritage touched hundreds of lives. My father-in-law received fifty years of dedicated, loyal love and care for himself, as well as for their children and home. I believe that my mother-in-law's goal for her five sons was for them to understand the importance of being honorable and dependable men raised to fight for the causes God fights for. Her five daughters where taught above all else to make Jesus their first love, and to be wise and discerning women in all of their decisions. Through sweet songs, she taught her 25 grandchildren that Jesus loves them. They also were advised to obey God and their parents, and to behave with good manners toward everyone. Friends, neighbors, and even those she hardly knew were treated with warm hospitality and with the compassion of a listening ear. The lessons that my mother-in-law taught me were how to live wisely and be pure in the Lord, to take care of my home, and to do good. She also taught me to be submissive to my husband, as the Bible explains it, so as not to bring shame on the word of God (Titus 2:4-5). All of this was done with such a sweet, loving spirit. I am now mature both in age and in my spiritual relationship with Jesus. I believe that it is my time to add to my family's Godly Heritage through the way my marriage is conducted and the type of mother I am to our children.

I could fill a book with precious stories of how this dear lady led person after person to the Lord. I am sure that each person whose life she influenced would say that it was the little things she did that made them pay attention to the way she lived. Whether you were just having coffee with her or sharing in a theological discussion on spiritual matters, Betty took every chance to tell you about her Lord and Savior. I have mentioned through the Mother in Love Series how much she loved to sing and how through the words of those songs she taught us many things. If I could sum up in lyrics what I think was the Godly Heritage she desired to establish for her family, it would be this song: *What a Friend We Have in Jesus*. Her life since she became a Christian in the early 1970s was lived as a friend of Jesus.

At her funeral were gathered about two hundred of her closest friends and family. People saw the peace and calm that her children felt because they knew that after a short battle with sickness, which could not have been won here, their mother was living in eternal victory with her King. There were definitely tears for the loss of such a special person, loved by so many. To me she was everything rolled up into one delightful package. She was my best friend, my counselor, my teacher, my spiritual mentor and one of the few people who said every time I called her, "I'll be right there." Because of her selfless love, she came and helped every time the children were sick or hurt or if I just needed to talk. How do you thank someone for all of that? She was an awesome mother-in-law and from the day I married her son, I felt like her daughter. I am filled with a flood of memories and a rush of emotions as I look back trying to re-cap this relationship. Of course, I cannot incorporate every detail of how blessed I am by this Godly Heritage I have become a part of. What I take away is celebrating the legacy that has been left by someone who followed Jesus and celebrated each breath He gave her.

I believe that we have an obligation to be the strong Godly role models the younger generations are watching. A Godly heritage means we teach others about God and strive to be the examples people will want to follow. From the relationship that was formed over the years between me and my mother-in-law, I learned that in other people we find assorted characteristics we would like to follow.

In Jesus, we find all the characteristics we should follow. Betty's spiritual legacy means this to me: be an example to all people in what you teach, in the way you live, in your love, your faith and your purity. (Paraphrased from 1 Timothy 4:12) Let nothing get in the way of establishing a Godly heritage. Celebrate all those lives who are watching you because you love Jesus! Believe me, because I know, if you live like that people will want what it is you have. Be ready to point them to Jesus.

Questions For Your Spirit

- What is your Godly Heritage? Was there someone who influenced your spiritual journey just because you noticed how they were living?

- If people were to follow your example, would it be easier for them to believe in Jesus? In what ways are you a good example? In what areas do you need God's help in becoming stronger?

- Even though people are watching us, we need to remember that, in order to establish a Godly heritage, we need to celebrate our relationship with Jesus. How will you follow the ultimate role model and stay centered on Christ in your life?

- Let's revisit some of the questions from the chapter. What type of heritage are you establishing for the generations to follow? What would you like people to say about you? Read Deuteronomy 12:7 again. How does this challenge you?

- Psalm 100:1-2 says, "I will sing of your love and justice. I will praise you, Lord, with songs. I will be careful to live a blameless life . . . I will lead a life of integrity in my own home." From reading this verse, what are some of the things we can do which will help establish a Godly heritage? How would this positively affect the lives of others?

Scripture to Celebrate

Romans 2:10, 2 Corinthians 13:11, Hebrews 10:20, Psalm (16:11 & 21:6 &78:5-6), 1 Kings 11:2-3

Genesis 17:9-14, Deuteronomy 28:1-6, Titus 2:12-15, Ezra 7:6-10, 1Samuel 3:13, John 15:19-21

What I Will Celebrate

What I Will Celebrate

Afterwards

Once we have come to a place where we celebrate all we have in Jesus, we are truly living the abundant life Christ tells us about. Throughout this book, we have been given many reasons why our situations can never keep us from experiencing God's presence. He is God, despite whatever we are going through, and He is there, ready to show us the way out and to Him. Getting to this point is a process; it begins with a desire to change, and it remains strong with the commitment to be faithful. The main objective of The Mother in Love Series is to bring light-hearted inspiration and Biblical truth to keep you encouraged as you walk these steps in your relationship with Jesus and with others. It has been a humbling privilege to share with so many people how God has blessed me and the work He has done in my life. I have said over and over that we all have stories and that is what I believe makes up life. We learn and grow by what we mean to one another and how someone's life touches us.

This is the final book of the Mother in Love Series. Each book contains a piece to a Christian lifestyle as it was taught to me. Even though we may reach new levels of awareness and experience more of God in our lives, we never reach the end of our maturity as followers of Christ until we reach heaven. We start at the beginning by giving our hearts to Jesus and walk the path close to His side until all we do is rejoice in how He has blessed our life. Spending daily time in prayer and in God's Word is the only way we will know Him better. This strengthens our faith and proves to us that our God reins above all the earth and everything in it. From the time the world was created, people have seen the earth and sky and all that God made. They can clearly see…His eternal power. (Romans 1:20)

Over the months it has taken me to put this material together, I began learning for myself what celebrating a friendship with Jesus is about. The word freedom kept coming to mind. Celebrating Christ's freedom in our lives is when we chose to live by faith and not by sight. (Hebrews 11:1) Once we can do that, all the negative bondage which wants to hold us captive to its misery can be released. The bondage can only be broken by submitting our hearts to the Lord. This type of celebration is intended for our souls and brings us new life in Christ. It is not like a party that we attend, have a good time at, and over the ensuing weeks and months forget. God wants this celebration to last in a joyous relationship with Jesus that we live every day. It caused me to think about the constant contentment that Matthew 6:25-27 speaks of. Here he refers to the carefree spirit of the birds of the air that we ought to imitate.

> Look at the birds of the air; they neither sow
> nor reap nor gather into barns, and yet your

heavenly Father feeds them. Are you not of
more value than they? And can any of you by
worrying add a single hour to your span of life?

For many of us, how many times has that passage brought comfort when we were unsure if we could handle the things we had to endure? The point for us to take is to celebrate that we can place our trust in God's unbounded love. We can become as free-spirited as the birds in the air with a safe refuge to land at. I pray that this book has brought you the encouragement to just live your life in the joy of serving and knowing the Lord. If you take only one thing away from the Mother in Love Series, I would want it to be that you know that we do not have to have it all together to go to God. He wants to clean us up from our own mess. There is nothing more beautiful to God than seeing a broken heart crying out for Him to fix it. This is what this series meant to me — learning that God does not want our perfection, but He wants to love us through our imperfections. I have shared many stories in these pages about imperfect people, including myself.

I leave you this one last thing to celebrate. Remember that at the end of your life, it wouldn't matter whom you have known other than Jesus. It would not matter what you have as long as you would give away your heart. It would not matter what you have done and where you have gone had you not been careful with how you lived. Therefore, you should love the Lord and your families, reach out to your neighbors, and serve those in need. If you have done this, you can celebrate because you lived your life well. Each book in the *Mother in Love Series* may have a different topic, but all has the same underlying message because there is only one thing we really need to get. I have a precious friend who says to me often, "You know, we have to tell them that people need the Lord in their life." I could not agree more, and I know it is true. I pray that you would know this need in your life and that you would ask God through His Son to fill it up overflowing. If nothing else, this series has been all about telling people about the great and mighty things God has done. May you draw nearer each day to our Lord and Savior Jesus Christ, and may you be richly blessed to celebrate each day by living it in His love!

About the Author

Mary's stories are taken from the lessons she has been taught in her life about the goodness of God and forging a practical relationship with the Holy Spirit. Her past struggles with an eating disorder inspired her to reach out in sharing a message of hope to others that recovery is possible through faith. Mary speaks openly about her struggles and the way God has blessed her life. That time period of struggle, which lasted several painful years, brought about personal growth, physical healing, and a new spiritual awareness. The experiences that both she and her family went through resulted in the blessing of starting her writing career. Mary published her first magazine article in April 2006 in *Spirit Led Woman Magazine* and published her first book in January 2008, titled *How a Mess Became a Message.* That book is actually her testimony of her family's walk with faith during her time of addiction to anorexia.

Her passion is speaking about what God can do in a life that is open to receive Him. Mary uses the Bible as a daily tool in which she applies its teachings in her life as much as possible. She has studied the Bible extensively.

Since 2001, she has taken classes at a Community Bible Study organization that is run at a seminary level intensity. Mary has also been part of small-group studies since 1993, providing her with the knowledgeable background she draws upon to write her daily devotions and reflections. Most recently in 2009-2010, she participated in an adult Life Time Education Application Program class at Hatfield Biblical Seminary.

Mary has been married since age 19 to the same wonderful man. They are blessed with one son and two daughters. The Barrett's live in North Wales, Pennsylvania where they enjoy living in close proximity to many relatives and friends. Some of the hobbies they enjoy are camping in their RV, swimming, going to the beach, visiting loved ones and enjoying God's creations; especially their Pug-Boston Terrier, Beau.

Currently, Mary is involved in the Mother in Love Conference Series which is based on her devotional books. She and her husband Tom are in the starting stages of planting seeds for a ministry that they pray God will grow in His time, called Titus II:1 Ministries. The vision of the ministry is to bring together all who seek a relationship with the Lord using a variety of outreach methods. This is in the very beginning stages, but they are ready to follow God as He leads.

Please feel invited to stay informed of all speaking engagements and publications on facebook. Go to either Mary Incollingo Barrett or to the Mother in Love Devotional/Conference Series page. If you want to personally communicate or book a speaking engagement for either a women's or church event, you can also e-mail at mtbarrett@verizon.net and can expect a quick response.

Moments To Rejoice

Moments To Rejoice